2000 Years of Building
- Chester's Architectural Legacy

Edited by Stephen Langtree and Alan Comyns

Published by

 The Chester Civic Trust

A SELECTION OF CHESTER'S BUILDINGS
FROM THE PAST 2000 YEARS

Dedicated to the memory of Mrs Gertrude Jones JP
founder member, and former Chairman and Vice President of
The Chester Civic Trust

 The Chester Civic Trust

Published by The Chester Civic Trust
Bishop Lloyd's Palace
51-53 Watergate Row
Chester CH1 2LE

Registered Charity No 504634

First published in the UK in 2001
Copyright © 2001 The Chester Civic Trust

ISBN 0-9540152-0-7

Design and origination: Kerry Maddrell Design Services
Printed by: The Printing House Ltd., Crewe

CONTENTS   PAGE

1.   Introduction   7
     Stephen Langtree

2.   Chester's history   9
     Eileen Willshaw

3.   1 - 400 Roman order   17
     Peter Carrington

4.   401- 1000 Saxon ghosts   31
     Peter Carrington

5.   1001- 1200 Norman stock control   37
     Oliver Bott

6.   1201 - 1500 Medieval 'boom town'   57
     Oliver Bott

7.   1501 - 1700 Dissolution, revolution, restoration   89
     Simon Ward and Oliver Bott

8.   1701 - 1800 Georgian decorum   109
     Derek Nuttall and Stephen Langtree

9.   1801 - 1900 Victorian exuberance   139
     Graham Fisher

10. 1901 - 2000 Expansion, demolition, conservation   181
     Peter de Figueiredo and Cyril Morris

11. Chester in the 21st century - 'a progressive historic city' ?   217
     Stephen Langtree

Sources   223

Acknowledgements   225

Index   227

Foreword by His Grace the Duke of Westminster OBE TD DL

As President of the Chester Civic Trust, I am delighted to write this Foreword to a book which celebrates not only the city's Millennium Festival but also the 40th Anniversary of the formation of the Chester Civic Trust.

There can be few greater cities whose buildings illustrate more clearly its continuous development over two thousand years. The year 2000 is undoubtedly a landmark in the passage of time and in the evolution of the City of Chester. It is appropriate, therefore, that this book should be a chronological history of the city, expressed through its many fascinating buildings.

Wherever we live and work, buildings have an immediate and lasting effect on our lives. Their size and style, and their relationship one with another, creates our environment and conditions our outlook. Chester is fortunate in having a 'human scale' in which there are buildings of great historical interest as well as architectural distinction. This selection of over 130 buildings and structures brings to life the atmosphere of Chester in different periods of history, from the Roman Wall in the first century AD to the very latest developments at the end of the 20th Century.

I hope this book will not only be a permanent reminder of the city's Millennium Festival but will also foster a sense of appreciation and pride in our inheritance.

His Grace the Duke of Westminster, Chairman of The Falcon Trust, unveiled a drawing by archaeologist Roland Harris illustrating the history of The Falcon, (May 1996).

FOREWORD
BY HIS GRACE THE DUKE OF WESTMINSTER OBE TD DL

As President of The Chester Civic Trust, I am delighted to write this Foreword to a book which celebrates not only the city's Millennium Festival but also the 40th Anniversary of the formation of The Chester Civic Trust.

There can be few greater cities whose buildings illustrate more clearly its continuous development over two thousand years. The year 2000 is undoubtedly a landmark in the passage of time and in the evolution of the City of Chester. It is appropriate, therefore, that this book should be a chronological history of the city, expressed through its many fascinating buildings.

Wherever we live and work, buildings have an immediate and lasting effect on our lives. Their size and style, and their relationship one with another, creates our environment and conditions our outlook. Chester is fortunate in having a 'human scale' in which there are buildings of great historical interest as well as architectural distinction. This selection of over 130 buildings and structures brings to life the atmosphere of Chester in different periods of history, from the Roman Wall in the first century AD to the very latest developments at the end of the 20th century.

I hope this book will not only be a permanent reminder of the city's Millennium Festival but will also foster a sense of appreciation and pride in our inheritance.

Westminster

CHAPTER 1

INTRODUCTION

STEPHEN LANGTREE

This book is the sixth and final part of our Millennium Festival '2000 Years of Building'. If you have bought it because you think it contains all the best buildings in Chester, then you might be wrong. Or perhaps you expect it to contain all the listed buildings in the city, in which case you're definitely wrong!

We have not set out to define what is 'best'. Architecture, like many other art forms, is a subjective matter which stimulates a healthy debate and differing opinions. Nor are we simply providing a selection of the 689 listed buildings in Chester. Whilst listing might be regarded as the most objective assessment of what is 'best', there are some Grade I listed buildings which are not in this book, and some unlisted buildings which are.

Instead, our aim is to provide a representative sample of the surviving evidence of almost 2000 years of occupation and development in Chester - a process which started with the Romans in the first century AD and continues to the present day. This architectural guidebook is but one component of a successful Millennium Festival which has celebrated Chester's unique legacy of buildings, structures and monuments from almost every period in its history.

Conceived and promoted by The Chester Civic Trust, the Festival has been an active partnership with Chester College of Higher Education, the Cheshire Society of Architects and Chester City Council. Staff from the Council's Archaeology and Heritage Departments have been willing contributors to this book, although most of the text and the majority of the photographs have come from members of the Civic Trust and the Chester Photographic Survey. These are people who are passionate about their city. People who love it for its size, its human scale and its character but, above all, for its history and heritage.

There were many reasons why we chose to celebrate the new millennium in this way. The year 2000 is undoubtedly a landmark in the passage of time and, by coincidence, it is also the 40th anniversary of the formation of The Chester Civic Trust. Our objective for the entire festival has been to interpret Chester's buildings in the context of time, unravelling some of the confusion between historical periods and architectural styles. This is why our guidebook is arranged as it is - in a chronological series of chapters, each covering one or more centuries in the long history of this city.

Of course, nothing is ever that simple. Chester's buildings are not always what they seem to be. Much of the fabric of our central streets is either a lot older or newer than it appears to be. Most confusing of all are Chester's famous 'black-and-white' buildings. The majority are genuine timber-framed structures, but from two quite different periods. The older ones date from the 17th century (both before and after the Civil War in the 1640s) but they are considerably outnumbered by the newer ones which date from the second half of the 19th century. The 'best' are arguably the older ones which have survived up to 400 years, but the most prominent and well-known of Chester's "black-and-white show" are equally important as outstanding examples of Victorian design and craftsmanship. These newer buildings are often only timber-framed façades on structures which are otherwise built in brick. Nevertheless, they should not be confused with the 20th century examples, with their 'mock-Tudor' features which are simply stuck onto buildings in a non-structural and over-sentimental parody of the past. You won't find any of those in this book!

The 'real thing' can be even more complicated than this. Many of Chester's buildings have been partially reconstructed, extended and remodelled several times over hundreds of years. The Cathedral is an obvious case in point, although some may not realise the extent of its Victorian transformation at the hands of Sir George Gilbert Scott. There are many other buildings, particularly along the Rows, which have fabric dating back to the 13th and 14th centuries but which have been substantially 'modernised' by the Georgians, or the Victorians, or both. Our general rule in compiling this book has been to place each building in the period from which there is the oldest surviving evidence. Subsequent rebuilding or extension is indicated against the 'Timeline' along the edge of each page.

All of the 132 buildings described herein were nominated by members of Chester Civic Trust and the general public. They include the forty buildings and structures which were chosen by a panel, involving our Lord Mayor and Member of Parliament, for the Millennium Festival Trail. Those buildings, like all the others in this book, are intended to be representative of almost every period in Chester's development through time.

With a myriad of archaeological remains and architectural styles from so many different periods, Chester is indeed a fine historic city. We hope that the following chapters will stimulate your appreciation and enjoyment of our heritage and inspire you to join the Civic Trust to help shape the future of this very special place.

CHAPTER 2

CHESTER'S HISTORY

EILEEN WILLSHAW

Chester owes its existence to its strategically important position on the Welsh border. The site, on a sandstone outcrop guarding the lowest crossing of the river Dee, was chosen by the Roman army for one of their three legionary fortresses in Britain. The city has been occupied continuously ever since.

The Roman fortress of Deva was founded towards the end of the 70s AD, to control the newly occupied areas of North Wales and the western Pennines. It became the base for a legion of between 5,000 and 6,000 soldiers and a large civilian settlement grew up outside the defences.

The port, situated just to the west of the fortress in the area now occupied by the Roodee or racecourse, became one of the busiest of Roman Britain.

The high degree of standardisation in the layout of Roman military bases assists in the reconstruction of the plan, although the position and function of many buildings remain conjectural. The defences were rectangular or 'playing-card' shaped and on each of the four sides was a gateway giving access to the major streets. Three of these streets met at a central crossroads in front of the military headquarters or *principia*. As well as the

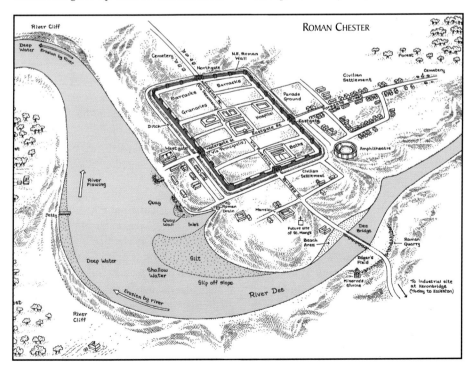

headquarters, there were the usual range of military buildings, including houses for the commander and other senior officers, barracks, bath-houses, granaries, workshops and hospital. Just outside the south-eastern corner of the fortress was the legionary amphitheatre.

The legacy of the Roman fortress has left its mark on the modern city. The major Roman streets and some of the minor ones have survived to the present day. Substantial sections of the northern and eastern City Wall are built on the Roman defences; both the Northgate and the Eastgate stand on the sites of their Roman predecessors.

Chester re-emerged from the Dark Ages in the 7th century, when it became part of the Saxon kingdom of Mercia. St John's Church is said to have been founded in AD 675. It may have served an early Anglo-Saxon community living to the east of the ruins of the Roman fortress. In AD 907 Chester was refortified as a burh, one of a network of fortified towns built during the reconquest of Mercia from the Danes. The survival of much of the Roman fortress meant that the framework for the new town already existed; the Roman defences were rebuilt and extended and the principal streets of the fortress were retained.

Chester's rapid growth in political importance and prosperity during the later Saxon period was largely due to the port, which thrived on the lucrative Irish Sea trade. This trade was financed by coins struck at the Chester mint, whose output in the 10th century was one of the greatest in Britain. A trading settlement grew up to the south of the old Roman fortress, along what is now Lower Bridge Street.

After the Norman Conquest, Chester held a key position on the Welsh border. William I established a castle in 1070 and this became the seat of a powerful earldom. The Norman Earls completed and extended the walls. A cathedral church was begun at St John's in 1075 and the great Benedictine Abbey of St Werburgh was founded in 1092. A causeway or weir was built across the river to provide water power for corn and fulling mills.

Chester's plan was essentially the one that had been inherited from the Saxons and the Romans before them. In general, the city centre buildings lay end-to the four main streets and were packed tightly together, although there were still many open spaces behind them. Continuous development along the street frontages was a significant factor in the evolution of Chester's most remarkable buildings: the elevated covered galleries known as the Rows.

Archaeological and documentary evidence suggests that a Rows system was largely in existence by the mid 14th century and that elevated walkways were an integral part of many buildings erected in the second half of the 13th century. They developed during a period when Chester was at the height of its economic prosperity. It was a flourishing port and military centre, with a powerful and

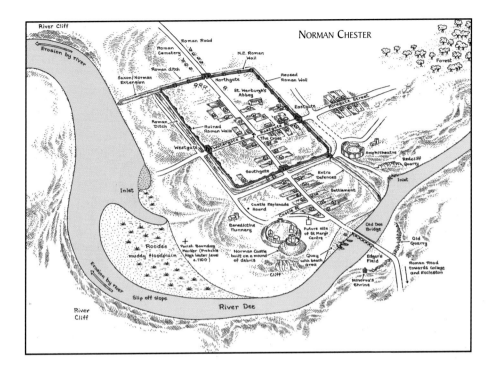

NORMAN CHESTER

wealthy community of merchants who embarked on an extensive rebuilding of the core of the city. Although recent studies have found no evidence of imposed town planning, the commercial advantages of buildings with shops at two levels were quickly recognised, contributing to the rapid development and subsequent survival of a system of building which is unique to Chester.

The Civil War of 1642-6 devastated the city. As an important royalist stronghold and the main port for the king's troops in Ireland, Chester was beseiged by parliamentary forces for over 18 months. In the later stages of the seige, the city suffered very heavy bombardment before being starved into surrender. War damage was considerable: all the suburbs were burned, the City Walls were in ruins, and not a street within the city escaped serious damage. Rebuilding took many years, continuing throughout the 1650s and '60s. Timber was used for the reconstruction of even the most important houses, including the Bear and Billet in Lower Bridge Street, a completely new town house built for the Earl of Shrewsbury in 1664. Brick was scarcely used in Chester until the 1670s when the first suburban brickworks was established south of the river. Reviving economic prosperity was reflected in the tremendous amount of new building which took place from the last two

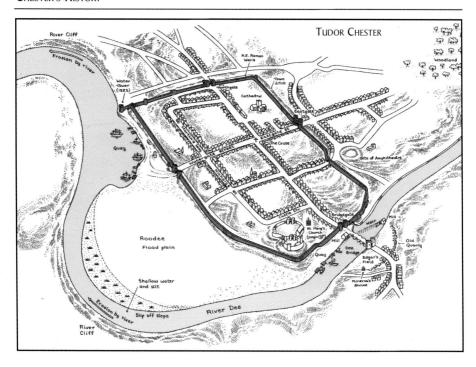

decades of the 17th century. This was particularly marked in fashionable Lower Bridge Street, where many of the local gentry owned substantial properties. Old timber houses were now replaced with brick mansions; others were simply encased or re-fronted. As part of this process the Rows which had extended along this street were lost.

Chester was typical of many other 18th-century county towns: prosperous, expanding, confident, and fashionable. It continued to develop as an important retail centre and flourished as a social centre for the leisured gentry and new professional classes. The port enjoyed a revival in the early years of the century. In 1735-6, eight miles of the river were

canalised and a new harbour was built at Crane Wharf. However, silting of the channel continued and, confronted by increased competition from the Port of Liverpool, the new Chester Canal was constructed in 1776-9.

Rebuilding continued throughout the 18th century until the principal streets were described as a 'motley and grotesque' mixture of decaying timber structures and classical façades in brick and stone. Terraces of smart town houses were built for the new urban gentry. Between 1754 and 1761 the Cathedral authorities redeveloped part of the Abbey Precinct as Abbey Square, building 'rows of genteel houses in the London style'. New developments also grew up on open land to the west of the city, at Nicholas Street and Stanley Place. Many of the best town houses were lost when the inner ring road was constructed in the 1960s. However, two major public buildings have survived: the Bluecoat School, a charity school of 1717, and the Royal Infirmary, which opened in 1761.

The City Walls, having long lost their military role, were converted into a paved walkway and the four medieval gateways were replaced. At the end of the 18th century, Thomas Harrison embarked on his great rebuilding of the crumbling medieval castle. He was also responsible for the Grosvenor Bridge, completed in 1832, three years after the architect's

death. To provide access to the bridge, a new approach road, Grosvenor Street, was laid down. This was the first significant change to Chester's Roman and medieval street pattern.

Until the end of the 18th century, most people still lived within the City Walls. During the Regency period, new suburbs began to develop overlooking the river at Boughton and at Curzon Park. However it was not until the population explosion of the 19th century that there was substantial suburban expansion. The population growth from 21,000 to 35,000 during the century was tiny compared to that of the major industrial towns, but inevitably it resulted in considerable new development,

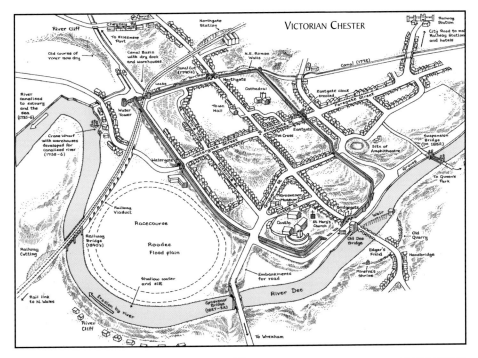

VICTORIAN CHESTER

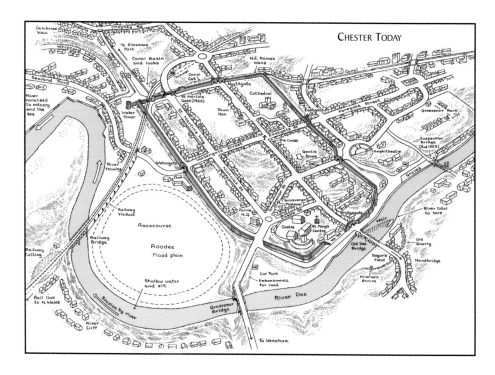

CHESTER TODAY

particularly to the north of the city, close to the railway station. Chester also had its share of squalid Victorian courtyard dwellings, the worst of which were packed behind the lavish new Town Hall.

Shopping and tourism were the mainstay of Chester's economy, particularly after the city was linked to the expanding rail network in the 1840s. Many new hotels were built in City Road, which was laid out as a new approach to the General Station in the 1860s. The Grosvenor Hotel opened in Eastgate Street in 1866. Eastgate Street, Chester's main shopping street, was favourably compared with London's Regent Street, whilst Browns' store became known as the 'Harrods of the North'.

The city was transformed by rebuilding in the second half of the 19th century. Notable new buildings included the Town Hall and the former King's School. The Victorian fashion for church restoration is very evident in the work of the local architect James Harrison, who restored or rebuilt most of the medieval churches, and in Sir George Gilbert Scott's full-scale restoration of the Cathedral. New sources of culture and recreation were also provided, with the chief benefactors being the Grosvenor family, most notably Grosvenor Park (1865-7), and the Grosvenor Museum (1886). However, it is the buildings of the vernacular revival which have made Chester so remarkable as a Victorian city. The contribution made by a group of local architects in developing a coherent style and identity for the city is now becoming more widely appreciated.

The first half of the 20th century was a relatively quiet period in Chester's development. The local predilection for the black-and-white style continued into and beyond the Edwardian period, notably in St. Michael's Arcade (1910-11) and the Royal Bank of Scotland building (1921). Major slum clearances behind the main streets took place in the 1930s, but with the exception of new buildings like St. Michael's Row and the Odeon Cinema, the city centre was little changed.

After World War II, housing became a major issue. Suburban housing estates rapidly expanded and Blacon was developed to the west of the city.

Post-war Chester confronted major changes - traffic management, the threat of comprehensive redevelopment, and inner-city decline. However, largely due to the conservation movement which began in the 1960s, Chester has changed far less dramatically over the last four decades than have many other historic towns. At the beginning of the third millennium, it is still possible to trace the legacy of 2000 years of development through Chester's buildings: this legacy and the changes which have taken place are all documented in the following chapters.

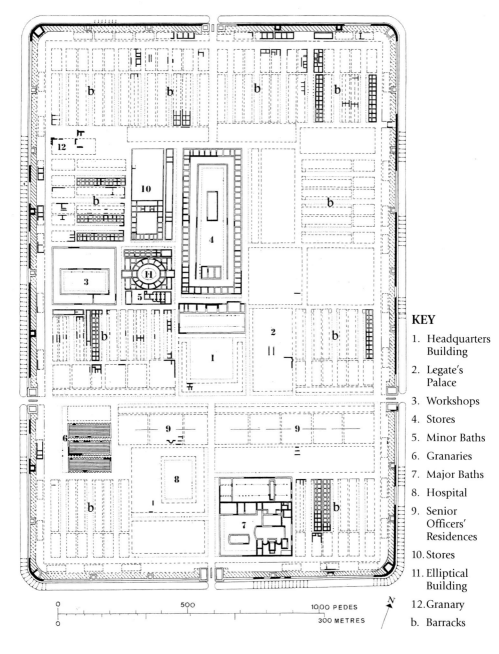

KEY

1. Headquarters Building
2. Legate's Palace
3. Workshops
4. Stores
5. Minor Baths
6. Granaries
7. Major Baths
8. Hospital
9. Senior Officers' Residences
10. Stores
11. Elliptical Building
12. Granary
b. Barracks

PLAN OF THE LEGIONARY FORTRESS OF DEVA C AD 235

CHAPTER 3

ROMAN ORDER
1 - 400

PETER CARRINGTON

There is little evidence that Chester was a significant place in prehistoric times. The city owes its origins to the recognition by the Roman army of its strategic position, between North Wales and north-western England, guarding the lowest crossing of the Dee and having a fine natural harbour. A legionary fortress was founded in the 70s of the 1st century AD to consolidate the conquest of this part of Britain.

There may have been earlier military occupation of the site, but this is uncertain. The location of the fortress indicates that access to the sea was always an important factor. The fortress was carefully positioned on a low sandstone ridge overlooking the head of the estuary and thus enjoyed a commanding position and good natural drainage. Named *DEVA* by the Roman authorities, the fortress was occupied first by Legion II Adiutrix, then by Legion XX Valeria Victrix. Occupation seems to have come to an end in the last decades of the 4th century.

In its essentials Chester fits in to the normal pattern of Roman military bases of the early Empire. In outline it was rectangular, with gateways on each side giving access to the major streets. Three of the streets met at the central crossroads, which was overlooked by the headquarters building (the *principia*) Around the periphery and along the main transverse street were the barracks, which would have housed 5,000-6,000 men when fully occupied. Much of the remainder of the space was occupied by other standard buildings: the commander's residence, granaries and other stores, workshops, hospital, and baths. However, Chester was rather larger than other legionary fortresses in Britain, at 24 hectares rather than 20, and contained a number of unusual buildings in its central area, especially the so-called Elliptical Building. These hint at a special purpose for the fortress - possibly an intention that it should serve as an administrative centre for the provincial governor, or as a base for the invasion of Ireland. With the exception of the baths, the buildings of the fortress were initially erected in timber. Reconstruction partly or wholly in local sandstone soon began, but this was a long drawn out process, with interruptions caused by the legion's commitments elsewhere. Roman fortresses were expressions of imperial grandeur as well as having a military purpose, and this is reflected in the monumental style of Chester's defences and major buildings.

The main approach roads to Chester were from London (*Londinium*), along Watling

Street, which entered through the south gate after crossing the river by a bridge just downstream of the site now occupied by the Old Dee Bridge, and from York (*Eboracum*), which entered through the east gate. A road led from the north gate down the Wirral, and the west gate gave access to the harbour.

Surrounding the fortress on all sides except, apparently, the north, was an extra-mural settlement, where soldiers' wives and a variety of traders would have lived. The settlement to the west and south, overlooking the river, seems to have consisted of high-quality buildings, including another baths near to present Watergate, and lodgings for the imperial postal service along what is now Castle Street. To the east there was apparently poorer-quality ribbon development along what is now Foregate Street. An amphitheatre lay just outside the south-east corner of the fortress. A cemetery lay west of the fortress on the site more recently occupied by the Royal Infirmary, and other scattered burials, especially cremations, have been found in Boughton, Handbridge, and along the Eaton Road.

The northern and eastern walls of the Roman fortress were incorporated into the medieval City Walls, and the lines of the main Roman streets have been perpetuated, with modifications, in those of the modern city. Eastgate Street and Watergate Street correspond to the *via principalis*, Bridge Street to the *via praetoria* and the northern part of Northgate Street to the *via decumana*. Some of the major

buildings have also influenced the modern layout. For example, north of the headquarters was a large oblong courtyard building, which stretched as far as where the Odeon cinema now stands. Its function is unclear, but it seems to have had a major impact on the later townscape, serving as the origin of the open space which is now Town Hall Square.

Apart from the walls and part of the amphitheatre, almost all the surviving Roman remains are to be seen below ground, in cellars and the like. Most of the Roman buildings that survived until the Middle Ages would have been demolished early in that period to allow the replanning of the city and their stone re-used in new buildings, especially the churches and the extended City Walls.

In-situ Remains   Page

Roman Walls   20

Roman Baths   22

Legionary Headquarters   24

Roman Amphitheatre   25

Roman Quay Wall   28

Minerva Shrine   29

ROMAN WALLS

As was the case with most Roman military sites of the early Empire, the initial defences of the Chester fortress consisted of turf banks crowned by timber palisades and punctuated by interval towers and gates. Gradually the towers and gates were replaced in stone, and a stone facing was added to the front of the rampart. The rear facing of the curtain wall is a medieval and later addition.

The northern and eastern walls were later incorporated in the medieval City Walls from St Martin's Gate / Morgan's Mount to the Newgate, and the best section that survives today is just east of the Northgate. This shows that the walls were built in a largely obsolete, but nonetheless monumental and very impressive style of large blocks with a projecting cornice (which corresponds to the height of the Roman wall walk). Usually, smaller stones were used and the surface rendered and painted to imitate larger blocks. The availability of easily worked sandstone at

South-east angle tower

Chester may have been a factor behind the choice of style. The present rounded profile of the walls is the result of the partial collapse of the stone facing as the supporting rampart behind settled over the centuries.

None of the Roman gates survive and only one of the corner towers can now be seen. The south-east

angle tower was first excavated in 1930 and displayed after re-excavation in 1951. The ground floors of the towers do not seem to have been used, being filled with the remains of the rampart into which they had been cut. However, there was a floor at the level of the wall walk. There may also have been a second floor above this; alternatively the first floor may simply have been roofed over.

The towers were built separately from the curtain wall, of smaller stones, and their upper stories rested on top of it. This was a cause of weakness, and the curtain wall eventually collapsed adjacent to the towers.

*

400

1000

1200

1500

1700

1800

1900

2000

ROMAN BATHS

39 BRIDGE STREET (BELOW 'SPUD-U-LIKE')

The internal baths lay in the southern part of the fortress, within a rectangular walled enclosure on the eastern side of Bridge Street. They consisted of a large exercise hall on the northern side of the complex and a suite of heated rooms on the eastern side. The south-western part was probably an open courtyard containing a swimming pool. A further suite of heated rooms ran along the south side of the exercise hall.

The aisled exercise hall was entered from a colonnaded portico along the street and contained a changing room at its western end and a small swimming pool. The eastern range consisted of three vaulted rooms. That nearest the exercise hall was a cold room; the other two providing increasing degrees of damp heat, akin to that found in Turkish baths. All contained small pools and basins. The three rooms along the south side of the exercise hall provided dry heat like that found in a sauna.

Because of its function, the baths were built of stone, brick and concrete from the beginning, whereas most buildings would initially have been of timber. The warm rooms were heated by a number of furnaces via underfloor ducts and, in the case of the sauna, by flues in the walls as well. Fragments of black and white mosaics have been found in the sauna, and it is probable that were mosaics in the other rooms as well.

The baths were erected at the time of the construction of the fortress, in the 70s of the 1st century, and like many other buildings in the fortress they seem to have been modified in the early 3rd century. They continued to be used, with periodic repairs and modifications, until the late 4th century. The post-Roman history of the building is inevitably vague, but much of it probably stood intact throughout the 'Dark Ages' and parts may have been occupied. Piecemeal demolition, starting from the Bridge Street frontage, probably started after the foundation of the late Saxon town and continued with the construction of undercrofts for the Rows

in the late 13th century and their later extension. Even so, the present-day Bridge Street frontage is largely built on the external wall of the Baths complex. The sheer size and massive character of the building meant that impressive remains survived, particularly in the backlands where they became buried as ground levels rose through rubbish deposition over the centuries.

Fragments of hypocaust have been known since the early 18th century and survive to be seen in the cellar of No 39 Bridge Street. Remains of the aisled hall were revealed in 1863 during demolition of the Feathers Inn. However, the true identity of the building was not recognised until much of it was exposed and destroyed after rapid recording during the construction of the Grosvenor-Laing Precinct in 1964.

Hypocaust in the basement of 12 Northgate Street (Miss Selfridge)

These were not the only baths in Roman Chester. A bath suite lay to the south of the Elliptical Building, while, as mentioned above, there was another substantial bath building near the Watergate. There are hints of further baths along Black Friars lane, again in the western extra-mural settlement. Another was attached to the lodging house for the imperial postal service, on the corner of Castle Street and Lower Bridge Street; and there may have been another to the south of the amphitheatre.

400

1000

1200

1500

1700

1800

1900

2000

LEGIONARY HEADQUARTERS
HAMILTON PLACE/NORTHGATE STREET

Overlooking the major crossroads of the fortress, stretching from what is now the Cross as far as Hamilton Place, was the Roman legionary headquarters building (*principia*). This was of the standard type, consisting of a hall with a courtyard in front.

The hall had a nave and two side aisles; behind it lay a range of rooms. Most of these would have served as offices, but the central one would have been a shrine containing a statue of the emperor and the standards of the legion. Below it was a cellar which served as a strongroom for the legion's pay. This was discovered during excavations in 1967-9 in advance of the building of The Forum and can be seen preserved *in situ* in Hamilton Place. Some of the column bases and fallen column drums from the northern aisle of the hall were discovered during the excavation of a cellar for No 23 Northgate Row West in 1897 and are preserved *in situ*.

The courtyard was surrounded by ranges of rooms, which may have served as armouries, with porticoes on both sides. In the middle of the southern range there would have been a large ceremonial entrance in line with a similar entrance in the hall and the shrine. Part of the courtyard surfacing has been found beneath St Peter's churchyard.

The headquarters was originally built in timber when the fortress was first founded, but very little is known about this first building. Early in the 2nd century it was rebuilt in stone. It then underwent alterations in the middle of the 2nd century, followed by major rebuilding in the 3rd century and was re-floored in the 4th century. As a result of the 3rd century rebuilding the courtyard and associated rooms were raised on a podium which would have dominated the crossroads, making the building look even more impressive.

Roman Strongroom (Hamilton Place)

ROMAN AMPHITHEATRE
LITTLE ST JOHN STREET

The first amphitheatre consisted of seating banks raised on a wooden framework enclosing the normal oval arena. It was replaced by a half-timber, half-stone structure. The higher seating banks were supported on a barrel vault spanning two concentric walls; the lower banks continued to be of timber. In this phase the arena was cut below the natural ground surface, rather than level with it, and the spoil from its excavation was redeposited to help raise the surrounding seating banks.

Far more is known about the stone amphitheatre than about its timber predecessor. Both enclosed the same size of arena, but the seating capacity of the timber structure has been estimated at only 2,000, that of the stone structure at 7,000. The stone amphitheatre had four major entrances giving access to the arena and eight smaller ones leading to the seating banks. A 'box' for dignitaries was found over the main east entrance, and there may have been another over the unexcavated west entrance. In the centre of the arena there seems to have been a timber platform. The projecting bases around the outside of the amphitheatre may have supported decorative columns.

One of the functions of the amphitheatre would certainly have been to provide a venue for military training and parades. However, on the north side of the arena of the stone amphitheatre was a small room which contained an altar dedicated to the Greek goddess Nemesis (Retribution). This argues that competitive and

bloodthirsty spectacles were also staged there. Shows put on by the aristocracy to impress the local population were part of the Roman way of life, and we may imagine that senior officers of the legion continued this practice while on their tour of duty at Chester for the benefit of the troops and local civilians.

The timber amphitheatre was probably built at the time of the foundation of the fortress. The rebuilding in stone is believed to have taken place cAD 100. Its later history is obscure, although it clearly underwent alterations. In post-Roman times enough of it survived to cause a large bend in the course of Little St John Street, which skirts its northern side. The hollow left by the excavation of the arena was not finally filled until the 18th century.

The amphitheatre was discovered by accident during building work in 1929 and first explored during controlled excavations in 1930-1 and 1934. At this time its survival was threatened by a road improvement scheme to remove the bend

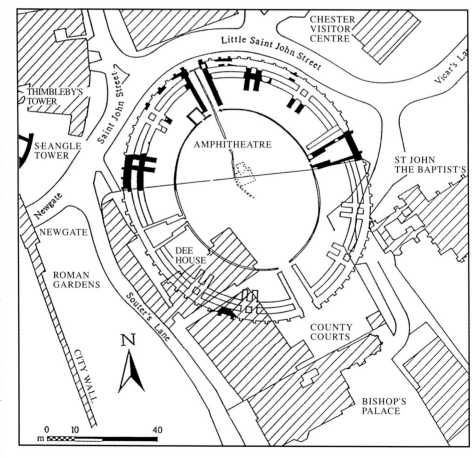

✱
●
400

1000

1200

1500

1700

1800

1900

○
●

2000

Part of the first large-scale excavation of the northern section in the 1960s.

in Little St John Street, which would then have run straight across the site. Thanks largely to the efforts of the Chester Archaeological Society this scheme was abandoned. The northern half of the amphitheatre as it appears today was excavated and displayed between 1957 and 1972. Proposals to excavate the remainder of the site have been made several times since then, notably in the mid-1980s and again in 2000. Many now see this as a long-term objective, but the presence of (Grade II listed) Dee House and a new County Court building above the southern half will ensure that the debate, and the controversy, continue well into the third millennium!

Outdoor concerts were staged in the Roman amphitheatre in June 1999 - possibly the first major event there for over 1600 years.

ROMAN QUAY WALL

NUNS ROAD

The Roman harbour undoubtedly lay to the west of the fortress, but its exact site is uncertain.

A section of masonry of Roman style in advance of the City Walls near Black Friars has long been identified as a quay wall. Its base lies below the present water table and its line has been traced northwards almost to the Watergate. However, no detailed investigations have been carried out since the last century, and the purpose of the wall needs to be reconsidered in the light

of what is now known about sea levels during the Roman period; it could simply have enclosed the western extra-mural settlement.

Fragments of what is thought to have been an early wooden jetty were found during the construction of the gas works off New Crane Street. The course of the tidal reach has changed dramatically over many centuries and it is possible that this jetty may have projected from the western, rather than the eastern, bank of the river.

Minerva Shrine

Edgar's Field, Handbridge

On the south bank of the river Dee in Handbridge are the remains of a large quarry which provided the stone for Roman Chester. On the eastern face of a small knoll left by the quarrymen is a very eroded relief of the goddess Minerva.

Minerva was the Roman goddess of war, knowledge, and craftsmanship, and so would have been the patron of the soldiers who worked the quarry. She was also the protector of travellers, and it was therefore appropriate that her statue should face the bridge which carried the main road south over the Dee.

Minerva was identified with the Greek goddess Athena and was often represented in art with the same attributes: helmet, shield, breastplate, and spear, together with Athena's special symbol of an owl. At Chester, Minerva is shown standing within a much-simplified representation of a temple, with an altar to her right. The opening to the right, known as Edgar's Cave, is possibly a natural fissure that was later enlarged. The relief may have survived the Middle Ages by being confused with one of the Virgin Mary and is now almost unique in western Europe.

1000

1200

1500

1700

1800

1900

2000

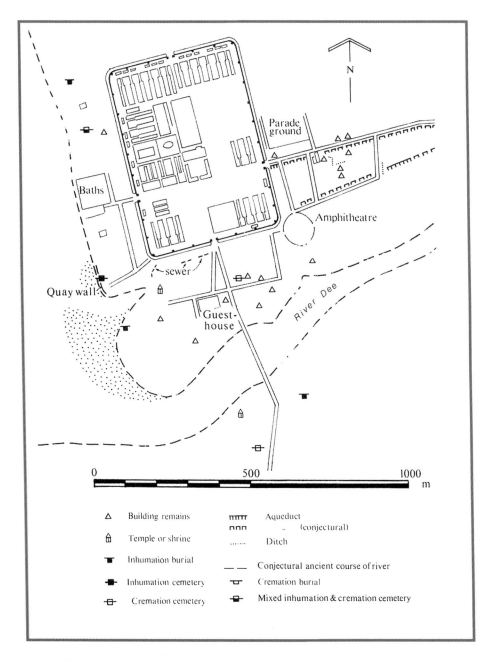

PLAN OF ROMAN FORTRESS AND CIVILIAN SETTLEMENT

CHAPTER 4

SAXON GHOSTS
401 - 1000

PETER CARRINGTON

Roman military occupation of Chester ended about AD 370 but direct rule of Britain continued, albeit with increasing difficulty, until AD 410. The country became divided into kingdoms founded on late Roman political arrangements. Chester remained in that part of the country which fell under 'British' rather than Saxon control, and centres of power were now often based on rural sites. Chester was largely abandoned, although it seems to have retained some importance and probably fell within the Welsh kingdom of Powys. It was probably the meeting-place for St Augustine and the British clergy (including monks from the large monastery at Bangor-on-Dee) about AD 603. In AD 616 Aethelfrith, ruler of the expanding kingdom of Northumbria, defeated the Mercians and their temporary allies from Powys at the Battle of Chester.

Chester eventually fell under Saxon control during the growth of Mercia in the 7th century. This growth was later symbolised by the construction in the middle of the 8th century by King Offa of the dyke that bears his name. By the end of the 9th century, the area around Chester was probably the only part of northern Mercia to remain in English hands after the Danish raids. The natural importance of Chester's position re-asserted itself in AD 907 when Aethelflaed, 'Lady of the Mercians' and daughter of Alfred the Great, founded a burh or fortified town here during the reconquest of the Danelaw and as a protection against Viking raids from the Irish Sea. Chester prospered as part of the new unified English kingdom and became one of the main centres of Irish Sea trade, with a flourishing mint. According to the Domesday Book, immediately before the Norman Conquest it contained 508 houses.

Until the late 9th century the buildings of Roman Chester must have gradually decayed, but occupation was clearly not intensive enough to obliterate them and impose new patterns. Indeed, areas inside the fortress seem to have been given over to cultivation or stock pens, while areas outside were ploughed. There may have been a church on the site of the legionary headquarters building - the site of the modern St Peter's - from late Roman times. St John's church was supposedly founded in AD 689 - soon after Chester had been incorporated into Mercia - although this date is disputed. Finally, what is now the Cathedral was originally a church dedicated to Saints Peter and Paul - a very early type of dedication - before being rededicated to St Werburgh in AD 907. It is not known where the population of Mercian Chester lived, but it may have been in the area around St John's church. Clear traces of new secular building are evident only from the time of the foundation of the burh in AD 907. There seems to have been an attempt to concentrate the population within the shelter of the fortifications. The old Roman defences were restored and may have had earth banks added at the north-west and south-east corners, extending them to the river. Burhs were usually laid out with rectilinear street grids, and this tendency probably accounts for the survival of Chester's main Roman streets. It is possible that the frontages of the main streets began to be built up by this time and the Roman buildings on the sites deliberately demolished, although the presence of medieval and later buildings make it difficult to find out. However, some late Saxon buildings seem to have been fitted around the Roman remains, in former courtyards or even across minor roads.

Outside the old fortress, a settlement sprang up along Lower Bridge Street. The churches dedicated to the Norwegian St Olaf (Olave) and the Norse-Irish Saint Bridget suggest the ethnic character of this part of the town. St Bridget's church was built on the site of, and possibly incorporated, one of the towers of the Roman south gate. There was also a bridge across the river Dee, probably a reconstruction of the Roman one.

Most of the buildings of this period, with the exception of churches, would have been of timber and so have not survived: the only traces are the post holes, floors and, for some of the later buildings, cellars, found during archaeological excavations. Nor can any Saxon work be seen in the churches, as their importance in later times meant that they were rebuilt many times.

400

1000

1200

1500

1700

1800

1900

2000

Chester as it might have appeared from the south-west in the late 10th century. In reality there would have been more houses - 508 are recorded in the Domesday Survey.
(Illustration by D Ashley and A M Beckett, courtesy of Chester Archaeology).

400

*
1000

1200

1500

Artist's impression of a group of
cellared buildings excavated in
Lower Bridge Street in 1974-6.
They were built in the late 9th or
early 10th centuries and may have
been of Scandinavian style.
*(Drawn by Peter Aleton, copyright Chester
Archaeology).*

1700

1800

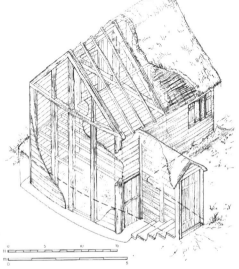

1900

Reconstuction of one of
the cellared buildings

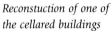

2000

SAXON CROSSES
(CHURCH OF ST JOHN THE BAPTIST)

A long with St Werburgh's, St John's was one of the major churches of Saxon Chester. As explained above, nothing of the original fabric is to be seen. However, in 1870, during reconstruction of the east end of the church, a number of late Saxon crosses were found that were presumably originally erected in the churchyard. They are now displayed in the north-west corner of the nave. These are in a distinctive style with round heads that is to be found around the coastlands of the Irish Sea.

Adjoining St John's church was the manor of Redcliff. This name suggests that the scarp behind the bowling green that lies between the church and the river originated as the face of a quarry where these crosses were made.

400

*
1000

1200

1500

1700

1800

1900

2000

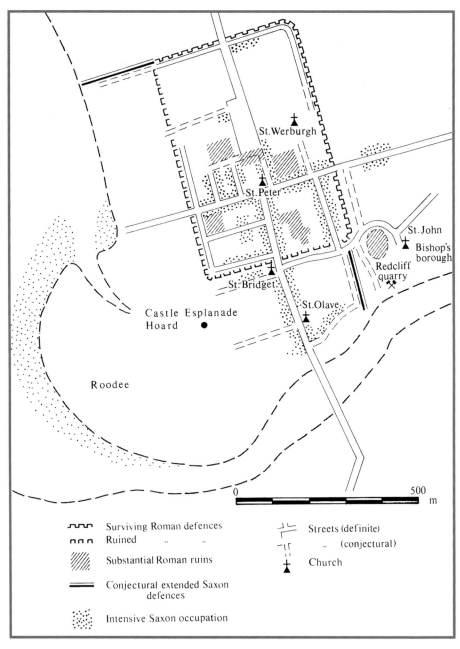

PLAN OF CHESTER IN THE 10TH CENTURY

CHAPTER 5

NORMAN STOCK CONTROL
1001 - 1200

OLIVER BOTT

The Domesday Book was prepared during the early 1080s to give William I an orderly register of the assets which fell into his hands when he had slain his rival Harold at Hastings, then seized the English throne. It describes Chester during the reign of Edward the Confessor, the last Saxon king to die in peace, as a well established and substantial town at the lowest bridgepoint across the River Dee: then it notes the havoc which William's men-at-arms wreaked there in the 1070s. Northerners saw William the Conqueror as a usurper rather than a legitimate victor, so they rose in revolt against his rule. Cestrians took part in the uprising and the king's response was swift and brutal. His troops burned down 205 of the 508 houses which they found in the town.

Agricola Tower

The vigorous and ambitious Normans had a clear goal. They found a town lightly built of timber, wattle-and-daub and thatch. They knew well how to rebuild in timber, but also in stone, for they had studied the ancient Roman structures which they found in France when they settled there as colonists. They were now the masters in England and meant fully to enforce their will. They saw no reason to conserve what their defeated forerunners had built.

Chester's medieval history has helped to mould the city's subsequent development. William ennobled his nephew

Hugh d'Avranches (Hugh 'Lupus') as Earl of Chester and gave him full authority to administer the shire. He initiated the building of the medieval City Wall so as to double the area of land already protected by the ramparts of the Roman fortress - and without delay he set about constructing Chester Castle. He refounded St Werburgh's Abbey, provided for the rebuilding of the church of St John the Baptist and the great weir to power the Mills of Dee.

Chester Castle

The Normans had perfected the feudal system which underpinned their military success across Europe. In peace and war each layer of society from monarch and barons down to villeins and bondmen owed sevice to its superiors and protection to its inferiors. Feudal power depended on castles which were the fortified residences of those concerned with government. Chester Castle was designed to be both the residence of the Earl and the judicial and administrative headquarters of the county. Hence it was occupied and managed quite separately from the town.

The burgesses and merchants continued to live and carry on business on the main streets which had first been the military viae of the Roman fortress, then the civil streets of the Saxon town. As leading citizens of a borough they were able to manage their affairs with some independence. The Benedictine Abbey of Saint Werburgh, then the precincts of an increasing number of churches, friaries and other religious houses were to occupy what now may seem a surprisingly large proportion of the land between the shopping streets and the City Wall: each such community lived according to their own monastic Rule, largely free of lay supervision.

BUILDING

PAGE

Chester Castle *(c1070)*   40

Church of St John the Baptist *(1080s)*   43

The Medieval City Walls *(c1075-1326)*   46

Chester Cathedral *(1092)*   49

Weir of the Mill of Dee *(1092)*   54

The Agricola Tower *(c1150)*   55

CHESTER CASTLE

CASTLE PRECINCT

Today, little remains of Chester's medieval castle, most of it having been removed by Thomas Harrison in his rebuilding between 1788 and 1822. No definitive history or guidebook to the castle has ever been published, but a full chronology and listing of all the standing structures is contained in a draft conservation plan for the castle prepared in 2001 for English Heritage. The castle area may have been fortified by the Mercian Queen, Aethelflaed, in AD 910, but in 1070 William I ordered the building of a full-blooded Norman castle. The plan, shown here, was of the typical motte and bailey design. The great grassy mound or motte, best seen from the City Wall just south-east of Grosvenor Road, would have been raised at once and crowned with a timber palisade. The stone walls of the inner bailey replaced the palisade some years later and the surviving Agricola Tower (*qv*), which flanked the entrance from the outer bailey, was built c1150. The inner bailey can be visited via the right-hand far corner of Castle Square. The ramparts facing the river are freely accessible but the Agricola Tower with its vaulted chapel with interesting ceiling murals is at present seldom open.

400

1000

*

●

1200

○

○

●

●

●

○

●

1500

○

●

○

●

○

1700

●

○

●

1800

(CHAPTER 8)

1900

2000

Plan of Chester Castle as it existed in the late Middle Ages

400

The medievel castle fell into disrepair and was restored several times during 700 years, the last occasion being during the Jacobite rebellion of 1745.

1000

The large outer bailey was demolished in 1770 to make way for the splendid Greek revival buildings of Castle Square when the former royal residence became the Cheshire Regiment headquarters, Shire Hall and Crown Court (see Chapter 8).

1200

1500

1700

Napier House (1830-32), the new armoury designed by Captain Kitson, standing above the south-east corner of the Castle walls.

1800

(CHAPTER 8)

1900

2000

c1080 • Listed Grade I • Scheduled Ancient Monument (ruins only)

CHURCH OF ST JOHN THE BAPTIST

VICAR'S LANE

Usually called St John's Church, the present building and adjacent ruins occupy one of the oldest religious sites in Chester. Evidence suggests that the first church may have been built here in the 7th century, and much of the building material is believed to have been derived from the Roman amphitheatre nearby. Probably during the 1080s the Normans began to rebuild the Saxon Minster which stood just outside the City Walls. The great new church was to become, for a time, the cathedral for Lichfield diocese. Mid 19th-century restoration has put a Victorian imprint on the exterior, but within, the mighty pillars of the nave, the lofty crossing, and the shortened chancel, all with simple round arches, take one back nine centuries. Once those were built, work ceased for a hundred years and the lighter pointed arches of the nave triforium and clerestory show how architectural style had changed before work resumed. The stained glass west window shows a half-mythical story of Chester's past.

Much more could and should be said about St John's Church as one of the oldest and finest buildings in Chester. Nothing of any greater antiquity survives (partly) intact and in use anywhere in this city. It is a sobering thought that this church, more than most in Chester, continues to serve the same purpose as it did nearly a thousand years ago!

400

1000

*

1200

1500

1700

1800

1900

2000

400

1000

1200

1500

1700

Like many of Chester's buildings its scale and fabric have changed markedly over the centuries but, unlike most, the best impression is now gained from inside rather than outside. Visitors may be surprised by the residual size of the nave and by its light, pinkish sandstone, which is altogether brighter than the inside of Chester Cathedral. St John's was once almost twice as long as the present church - stretching back into what is now Grosvenor Park. Some evidence of this grandeur is still visible from the ruins at the east end, but even these do not reveal the full extent of the former collegiate church.

1800

1900

2000

St John's Church has never had much luck with its towers. The building is thought to have suffered serious damage c1470 by the collapse of the (supposed) central tower, and again in 1572 and 1574 by the partial collapse of the north-west tower. More recently, the same great west tower, which was a prominent landmark on Chester's skyline, collapsed in April 1881. The north porch was destroyed but rebuilt by John Douglas in 1882. There has never been enough money to rebuild the tower, so St John's stands flanked by ruins at each end, but is no less magnificent within.

400

1000

1200

1500

1700

1800

1900

2000

THE MEDIEVAL CITY WALLS

Up to 1066 Chester relied for defence on its 900-year-old Roman ramparts, which had gradually fallen into decay and, at least until AD 907, were largely neglected. During the late 11th century William the Conqueror set about the first stage of their renewal. He extended the fortified enclosure westward from Nicholas Street and St Martin's Way to the steep edge of the Roodee and southward from Pepper Street and Cuppin Street to the River Dee, enclosing the site of his new castle.

During the Middle Ages, impressive defended gateways were built at the Eastgate, Bridgegate and Northgate. The Watergate, which led out to the main Port

400

1000

* * * *

**

1200

1500

1700

●

○ 1800

1900

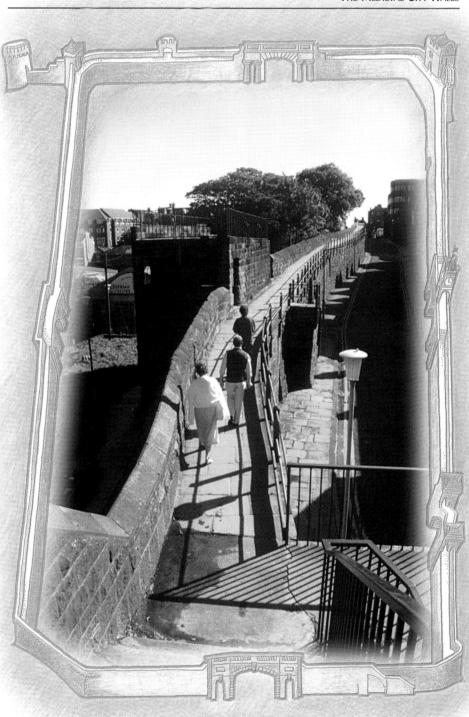

○ 2000

400

1000

****
****
1200
**

1500

1700

●

1800

1900

○
2000

The siege of Chester by Parliamentary forces lasted intermittently from November 1644 until the city surrendered in February 1646. Tremendous damage was caused to the walls. A repaired breach just south of the Newgate demonstrates the intensity of the bombardment: cannon ball marks can still be seen in the south-eastern wall.

The devastation caused by the conflict meant that attempts to repair the wall were inevitably half-hearted. It was not until the beginning of the 18th century that the City Corporation began to repair the walls and convert them into a promenade.

These improvements were abandoned temporarily during the Jacobite scare of 1745, but by the end of the century the walls had been transformed into a peaceful promenade. Most of the medieval towers had been taken down for the convenience of pedestrians, and the four medieval gateways were removed and replaced by arched bridges.

of Chester, was a simple arched opening through the walls. Eastgate, the main entrance to the city, was a tall tower with four projecting turrets and low flanking towers. Stylistic similarities to the King's Gate at Caernafon Castle suggest that it was built in the early 14th century.

Keeping the walls in good repair was a constant preoccupation for the city authorities. From the later Middle Ages, the upkeep of the wall was the responsibility of the Muringers, two elected officials who collected a special murage tax levied on exports. However, by the mid 17th century the walls were in very poor condition and at the outbreak of the Civil War in 1642 they were extensively repaired.

CHESTER CATHEDRAL
ST WERBURGH STREET

Originally St Werburgh's Abbey, this is now the Cathedral of Christ and the Blessed Virgin Mary. Medieval monasteries were centres of almsgiving, worship, learning and culture, guardians of orthodoxy, and a source of loyal and capable men from France and England on whom the king depended to administer his realm. Medieval Chester's position at

the gateway to North Wales made it a vital centre of activity for both church and state. In 1092 Hugh, 1st Earl of Chester, founded St Werburgh's Abbey on the site where a Saxon college of secular canons had already served the community for many years.

On the dissolution of the monasteries during the 1540s Henry VIII was to transform the Abbey into a Cathedral. The Abbey and Cathedral have endured many alterations century by century ever since, but the great church and the monastic buildings which adjoin the cloister remain one of the best preserved examples of a Benedictine abbey in Britain.

400

1000

1200

1500

1700

1800

1900

2000

Several internal Norman features survive. Most prominent is the north transept (early 1100s) of simple round-arched sandstone, eroded by time. In the floor of the north choir aisle, close to the corner of the north transept, the circular base of a great Norman pier and an upturned capital are exposed. Barclays Bank hides the exterior of the north-west tower, but its Norman interior (c1140) can be seen from the north-west corner of the nave.

In the cloister the wall to the nave has late Norman blank arches. The early Norman round-pillared and groin-vaulted undercroft to the abbot's lodging stands west of the cloister, accessible from the cathedral shop, but the abbot's Norman chapel above is not normally open to the public.

Among later medieval features of the Abbey and Cathedral the following are of special interest: The Lady Chapel beyond the choir (c1260-80) shows how early Gothic masons delighted to supplant massive Norman masonry with slender stone shafts and rib-vaults to create an airy, welcoming chamber which contains the medieval pilgrims' shrine to St Werburgh, reerected after long lying buried beneath Cathedral Green. The Chapel is redecorated in the manner of the 13th century.

Between the Lady Chapel and the transepts the richly carved oak choir stalls (late 14th century) are amongst the finest in England, with notable decorations on the misericords. East of the cloister are the very beautiful Early English vestibule and lofty chapter house (early 13th century). North of the cloister the monastic

400

1000

1200

1500

1700

1800

1900

2000

400

1000

1200

1500

1700

1800

1900

2000

refectory is now the cathedral restaurant. The raised stone pulpit (c1300) which projects from the south wall is evidence that the monks ate in silence while a Brother in the rostrum read them sacred texts.

The nave floor was paved for the first time in 1600 but, otherwise, there was no building work or restoration at Chester

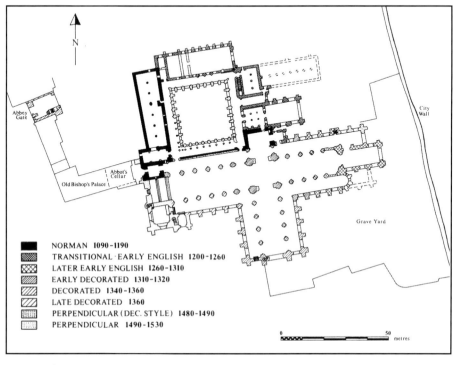

NORMAN 1090-1190
TRANSITIONAL EARLY ENGLISH 1200-1260
LATER EARLY ENGLISH 1260-1310
EARLY DECORATED 1310-1320
DECORATED 1340-1360
LATE DECORATED 1360
PERPENDICULAR (DEC. STYLE) 1480-1490
PERPENDICULAR 1490-1530

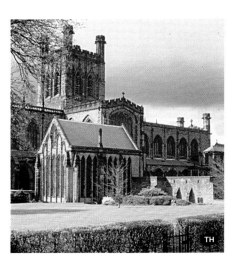

Cathedral from about 1537 to 1818. Damage during the Civil War in the 1640s went unrepaired, and in 1696 the building was described as 'miserably ragged on the outside'. Restorations by Harrison and Hussey in 1818 and 1843 respectively were followed by a major transformation at the hands of Sir George Gilbert Scott between 1868 and 1876. He entirely recased the worn exterior adding, in the process, some fanciful embellishments which radically affected the Cathedral's appearance.

Centre, well-illustrate Dean Smalley's many achievements and his belief in 'continuity with change'.

Controversy was again stirred in 1997 with the renewal of the nave floor, but this, along with new windows and a new Visitors'

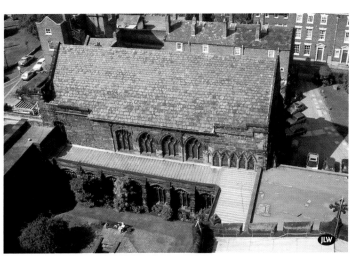

400

1000

1200

1500

1700

1800

1900

2000

WEIR OF THE MILL OF DEE
OR THE 'NORMAN WEIR'

In 1092 Hugh d' Avranches, 1st Earl of Chester, endowed St Werburgh's Abbey with the right to build a corn mill by the Dee Bridge. All that remains is the often-repaired weir and the adjoining salmon leap, which suggest the importance of fish and locally grown grain in the medieval diet. The mill was of

exceptional size, serving the people of Chester and the ships which thronged the port. By the late 13th century when Edward I was building his castles in North Wales the mill had six waterwheels and its annual rental was £200 - perhaps more than £500,000 in present terms. All Cestrians, by then, were obliged to have their corn ground there and the 'Miller of Dee' could afford to be 'jolly' when his business practices were little short of extortion.

In 1356 a lease for the mills bound the Crown to maintain the weir. In 1601 a large part of the causeway collapsed under the force of flood water. Repairs were made, only to be followed by deliberate acts of sabotage during the siege of Chester in the 1640s.

The Wren family purchased the mills from the Crown in the late 18th century and operated them until they were acquired by the Corporation in 1895. Destroyed by fire, the mills were finally demolished in 1910 and made way for a hydro-electric generating station (*qv*). The Weir was raised slightly at that time and although it no longer serves its original purpose it maintains water levels upstream and protects the water-works from saline intrusion.

Photo Survey

THE AGRICOLA TOWER
CASTLE PRECINCT

400

1000

The large red sandstone tower in the Castle courtyard, variously known as Julius Caesar's Tower, Julius Agricola's Tower, and The Agricola Tower, has no known Roman connections, although Roman remains have been found on the Castle site. It was built c1150 as the gate tower for the inner bailey of the castle, but the openings were walled up less than a hundred years later when a new gateway with two drum

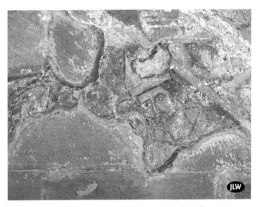

A fragment of the medieval wall paintings, showing the head of the Bishop of Adana (Southern Turkey)

1200

1500

towers was built. The medieval fabric was re-faced in sandstone by Thomas Harrison during his re-building of the Castle in 1818 (*qv*).

The Tower has three floors, reached by a stone staircase contained within the wall. The ground floor is a vaulted crypt. The first floor is the Chapel of St Mary de Castro (St Mary's in the Castle), built 1181-7. The walls of the Chapel bear traces of some very important medieval wall paintings which are believed to be the work of an artist in the court of King Henry III who took over the Castle in 1237. Now largely obliterated, the delicacy of the remaining images is protected by restricting public access. The Chapel is seldom used today, but the font there is still available for christening children of the Cheshire Regiment.

1700

1800

1900

2000

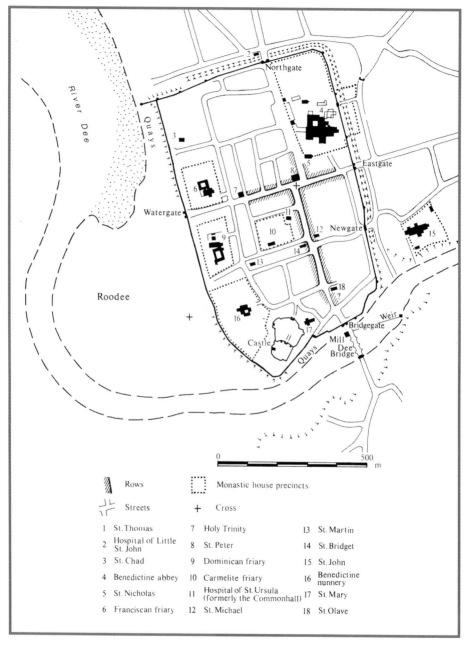

PLAN OF CHESTER IN THE MIDDLE AGES

CHAPTER 6

MEDIEVAL BOOM TOWN
1201 - 1500

OLIVER BOTT

The map shows something of the ownership and use of land in Chester during the Middle Ages, with principal buildings and the location of the Rows.

Buildings which survive from this period include fortifications, a number of churches and the Old Dee Bridge, the masonry successor to earlier timber bridges; but perhaps the greatest medieval gift to future generations of Cestrians has been the raised shopping galleries called the Rows. The extension to the City Walls initiated by William the Conqueror would have allowed the Saxon town to double in size under the Normans; but the undercrofts of only two merchants' houses within their protection have features dating from before 1260. Neither is easy to see and appreciate, but the ceiling beams in the undercroft of 34 Watergate Street (now 'Booth Mansion') date from between 1260 and 1280, and are more practical to view.

In 1277 a new epoch dawned which attracted wealth and skills enough to encourage the gentry and merchants of Chester to rebuild their town houses. Edward I chose the town as the base for his seven-year campaign to subdue North Wales: immediately thereafter Chester became the gathering-point for the engineers and craftsmen who built the chain of great castles from Flint to Harlech

which were designed to secure the land he had gained. The summer months were the only period fit for such work, so masons and carpenters, supervisors and labourers would winter in Chester, ready to take on any commission which they were offered.

Phoenix Tower

The boom in business which the huge campaign of castle-building generated evidently brought enough extra trade to enable the merchants of Chester to renovate or renew their homes. The choice which they made to adorn the fronts of their houses with open galleries overlooking the street matched the practice in other towns. The coincidence was that so many householders had means enough and a powerful desire to join the fashion at the same point in history. The unique circumstances were that ground levels sloped from the back to the front of these buildings and, although each gallery was privately owned, all the residents agreed to forego the privacy which partitions between neighbours' properties would have provided. Apart from the architectural curiosity of the Rows, the benefit is that Cestrians and visitors have been free for seven centuries to walk through sheltered galleries almost from one end of town to the other.

It is not now practicable to see any medieval town house as a whole, except the Blue Bell restaurant in Northgate Street; but in several other houses described and illustrated in this chapter - now cafes,

restaurants, winebars, the Old Kings Head Hotel, the Falcon and Boot inns and a number of shops - a visitor may easily examine either the undercroft a few steps down from the street or the upper storeys accessible from the Row. During the Middle Ages the undercroft was most commonly used as a warehouse and showroom. The merchant's office, the great hall and private chambers were at Row level and above.

Of the features shown on the map at the head of this chapter, the City Wall is well worth walking, although it was stripped of most defensive features after the Civil War. The Castle, although from Grosvenor Street partly concealed behind the far right corner of Castle Square, repays a visit for Agricola's Tower and the view across the Dee from the south rampart. Of the churches the Cathedral and its monastic buildings, St John the Baptist, St Mary on the Hill and St Peter are the most interesting. The Cathedral Close and viewpoints nearby on the City Wall show how differently the Church and the burgesses have developed their land. The north side of Watergate Street has the Row least altered since the end of the Middle Ages.

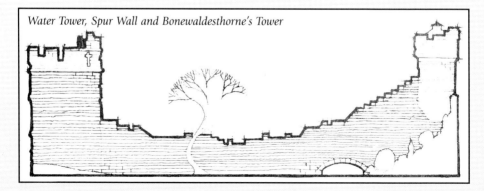

Water Tower, Spur Wall and Bonewaldesthorne's Tower

BUILDING   PAGE

The Rows *(13th century onwards)* — 60

The Old Kings Head Hotel *(1208)* — 63

The Falcon Inn *(c1215)* — 64

Booth Mansion *(1260-80)* — 66

Three Old Arches *(c1270)* — 68

Phoenix Tower *(c1280)* — 69

Abbey Gateway *(c1300)* — 70

Browns' Crypt *(c1300)* — 71

Watergates Wine Bar *(c1300)* — 72

St Nicholas's Chapel *(c1310)* — 73

Water Tower & Spur Wall *(1322-26)* — 74

Shuttleworths' Crypt *(c1330)* — 75

38 - 42 Watergate Street *(c1335)* — 76

St Peter's Church *(c1350)* — 78

St Mary on the Hill *(c1350)* — 79

Anchorite's Cell *(1363)* — 80

Bookland's Crypt *(1365)* — 81

Leche House *(c1375)* — 82

The Old Dee Bridge *(c1387)* — 84

The Blue Bell *(c1470)* — 86

The Boot Inn *(c1480)* — 87

1

13th century onwards • Listed as part of each building

400

1000

1200

**
**

1500

1700

1800

1900

2000

THE ROWS

Sheltered galleries or 'Rows' raised above street level link almost all the properties - and have proved a popular and profitable amenity for seven hundred years. The lie of the land may have sparked the concept. The main streets were still approximately at the level of their Roman forerunners, but much of the ground behind the buildings was higher than the streets because of the build-up of rubble and rubbish during the Dark Ages - so the lowest floor of a new building need be only a few steps down from the street if the next floor was to be level with the back yard. Most towns did

not have that advantage, so their undercrofts were deep cellars. A merchant's warehouse or showroom occupied the lowest storey or undercroft. The next floor at Row level had office and shop at the front, increasingly with a private chamber above. The hall stood immediately behind the shop and office. It was the principal household room, lofty and often open to the roof. Where a house was only one plot (c 5m) in width the hall stretched back at right-angles from the street. Broader houses would have had halls parallel with the street. The kitchen would have been to the rear, sometimes set apart in the yard.

400

1000

1200

**

1500

1700

1800

1900

2000

400

1000

1200

**

1500

1700

1800

1900

2000

A remnant of the Rows system in Lower Bridge Street

In practice the use of premises was often less tidy. If the householder was not a merchant the undercroft might be used as a tavern, with no access to the Row; the office and shop between the Row and hall might be let off as an independent business. Party walls of the undercrofts were of stone to prevent the spread of fire from one to another. The floor between undercroft and Row storey was often packed with rubble as a firestop. Forty-seven undercrofts retain enough medieval structure to establish their origin, of which eight good examples can be seen and four are described in this book. The grandest houses were of stone throughout, proof against neighbouring fires. Enough of the structure of four of them survives to establish their original form.

The remodelled 'Dark Row' (1992) at the corner of Eastgate Street and Northgate Street

THE OLD KINGS HEAD HOTEL

48 AND 50 LOWER BRIDGE STREET

Also called Ye Olde Kings Head. This originated as the house of Peter the Clerk, administrator at the Castle, from which the Earl of Chester governed the County Palatine on behalf of the king. The painted stonework facing Castle Street, beneath the bull-nosed oak joist-ends, may date from that period. The timber-framed frontage to Lower Bridge Street is 16th century, restored 1930s, and the main public rooms date from the 15th century. Most properties in Lower Bridge Street used to have first floor Rows, largely closed to the public in the 18th century. The line of braced oak posts in the restaurant above the bar shows how the former Row walk was included in the great hall c1740. The medieval post which is recut as a Tuscan pillar in the north-east corner points to the classical taste of the renovating Georgian proprietor.

The premises were first licensed 1717, since when the lower street frontage has been altered on several occasions. The building was heavily restored in the 1930s and again in the 1960s, when some rather unsympathetic changes were made to the bar areas on the ground floor. Nevertheless, having been continuously occupied and generally well maintained, the Old Kings Head was the only building of its kind in the Bridgegate area not to require the Council's intervention during the conservation programme of the 1970s.

TH

400

1000

1200

*

1500

1700

1800

1900

2000

THE FALCON INN
6 LOWER BRIDGE STREET

The Falcon forms part of a once much larger town house which extended further south along Lower Bridge Street. Behind the frontage, a massive 'great hall' ran parallel to the street. Later in the 13th century the house was substantially altered; the great hall was rebuilt and an elevated Row gallery was incorporated, similar to those elsewhere in Chester's main streets.

The oldest timbers are to be found in the Falcon's undercroft (now the beer cellar), which was once a warehouse-cum-workshop with a doorway and windows facing onto Lower Bridge Street. A heavy supporting beam has been tree-ring dated to around 1250, while two other timbers are even older and may have been salvaged from the roof truss which spanned the original great hall. Most of the stonework is late 13th century from when the house was recast, and the visible timberwork is largely 16-17th century.

In 1643 the householder Sir Richard Grosvenor was the first man successfully to apply to enclose his Row - he and his family had to live here because he served on the Royalist garrison and he stated that the space which the Row occupied made the house too small for their needs. The 13th-century stone piers in what is now the front bar of the pub are therefore part of the front of the house before enclosure of the Row, while the timber partition which runs through the seating area is a remnant of the late medieval shopfront in the Row.

Licensing records show that the Falcon was used as an inn from 1778 until 1878. In the following year it was restored by John Douglas and reopened as a temperance house - hospitality without the alcohol!

By the 1970s the Falcon was empty, derelict, and propped up to prevent collapse. The Falcon Trust was set up in 1979 to save the building. Funds were raised from several quarters and restoration work began in 1980 under the direction of Donald W Insall & Associates. Meanwhile the building has been donated

to the Trust by the Grosvenor Estate and was reopened by His Grace the Duke of Westminster in May 1992. Thus, ably restored, the Falcon is now a picturesque and interesting inn.

400

1000

1200

1500

1700

1800

1900

2000

400

1000

BOOTH MANSION
28-34 WATERGATE STREET AND 28-30 WATERGATE ROW

This building now looks like a fine Georgian house, but the interior shows a very different face. The mansion stands on the site of two medieval town houses. It retains much of the structure of the eastern one, a prime example of a 13th-century stone-built Row house, but because the whole building is now in commercial use there is no general public access. The only readily visible medieval features are the two chamfered stone arches which span the Row walk. The innovative Georgian frontage of 1700 projects forward from its neighbours and is slightly angled so that it can be seen in perspective from the Cross, an artifice which enhances its prominence in the street scene but led to the imposition of a fine (of £10 and five shillings annual rent) for the encroachment onto City-owned land.

Alderman George Booth, like other property owners similarly convicted, chose to pay rather than demolish the front of his fine new house.

Booth died in 1719 and soon afterwards the gentry and professional classes transferred their allegiance from the Exchange to the more genteel surroundings of Booth Mansion. Fashionable balls and entertainments were held in the Assembly Room above

MP

1200

*

1500

1700
●

1800

1900

○
2000

Row level until the 1770s when purpose-built accomodation was provided at the 'Talbot' in Eastgate Street. The Talbot itself was rebuilt and renamed the 'Royal Hotel', which it remained until 1866 when it was rebuilt again as the Grosvenor Hotel.

Cut-away illustration of the two medieval town houses showing the 18th century facade across the westernmost property. (Painting by Graham Holme, courtesy of The Chester Rows Research Project)

400

THREE OLD ARCHES
48-50 BRIDGE STREET AND 48-52 BRIDGE STREET ROW

1000

This building has perhaps the earliest shop front to survive in England. The 13th-century stone frontage of the undercroft and Row storeys is still clearly visible, though now framed by newer brickwork. The undercroft has a central doorway with a window-opening at each side, surmounted by three chamfered stone archways to the Row walkway. Early 14th-century enlargements took in two plots to the south, one of whose undercrofts survives. Behind the Row are parts of the largest example in Chester of a medieval stone-walled hall, set parallel with the Row. For much of the 20th century the shop below the Three Old Arches was the well-known and much admired William Jones' high-class grocers. Owen Owen took over in the 1960s and

1200

*

•

1500

amalgamated the premises with those of Richard Jones next door to create a department store. Nevertheless, the smells of freshly-roasted coffee, cooked meats, and cheeses continued to waft from the doorway until closure in January 1999. The premises have since been sub-divided and carefully refurbished, including new steps up to the Row just south of the Three Old Arches.

1700

•
1800

o
1900

o
•
2000

PHOENIX TOWER

CITY WALLS

Also called King Charles' Tower. This was the north-east corner tower on the medieval City Walls but, stripped of its defensive features after the Civil War siege of Chester, it was reused as a meeting room for several of Chester's Guilds. The main surviving medieval feature is the rib-vaulted octagonal chamber at the level of the Walls footway.

Probably of late 13th century origin, the tower is believed to have been called Newton's Tower during the Middle Ages. It was refurbished and altered in 1613 to become the meeting place of the Painters, Glaziers, Embroiderers, and Stationers Company, whose emblem was a phoenix - hence its name.

The alternative name of King Charles' Tower is derived from the events of 24 September 1645 when King Charles I stood on this tower and witnessed his defeated army being pursued from the battlefield at Rowton Moor.

The tower, which was largely rebuilt in 1658 and has been repaired several times since, is best seen from the canal towpath; its slender 21 m (69 ft) high circular form is particularly attractive.

400

1000

1200

✳

1500

●

●

1700

1800

1900

O

2000

400

1000

ABBEY GATEWAY
NORTHGATE STREET

1200

*

1500

1700

This archway, which formed the main entrance to St Werburgh's Abbey precinct, was built of warm red sandstone during the period when masons building Edward I's castles in North Wales were probably available to work in Chester during the winter months. The arched gatehouse led to a courtyard of buildings such as the abbey bakery and brewhouse, which were redeveloped as Abbey Square by the Dean and Chapter during the 18th century to house Cathedral staff.

The lower, medieval structure has a vehicular archway and a smaller pedestrian archway to the south. The roof within is common to both archways, being a three panel vault with hollow-chamfered diagonal and ridge ribs - similar to those in the undercroft at Browns of Chester (qv). Though appearing much older, the stone stairway against the south wall is probably c1800 when the upper part of the gateway was rebuilt. There are three rooms at first floor level, off a central passageway leading from a narrow spiral staircase at the south end. The room which faces Town Hall Square is the largest of the three and still has within it the ranges of wooden cupboards and other evidence of its former use as a robing room. The narrow stone staircase continues up to an attic room with a window facing east onto Abbey Square.

1800

1900

2000

BROWNS' CRYPT
28-30 EASTGATE STREET

This occupies a fine sandstone undercroft of four rib-vaulted bays surviving unaltered in the otherwise 19th- and 20th-century basement of Browns' department store. The undercroft lies immediately behind the Gothic revival stair-tower on the façade of the store (*qv*).

The internal length of the undercroft is 12.95m (42ft 6in) which, interestingly, is the same as that in Bookland (12 Bridge Street, *qv*) and in a contemporary building in Shoreham in Sussex. Investigations carried out for 'The Rows Research Project' - now fully described in *The Rows of Chester* (1999) - suggest that the undercroft can be dated between 1290 and c1320 from the distinctive sunken chamfers on the door jambs.

400

1000

1200

*

1500

1700

1800

●

1900

○

2000

400

1000

1200

*

1500

1700

1800

1900

WATERGATES WINE-BAR
11 WATERGATE STREET

This extremely fine sandstone undercroft has two naves of four vaulted bays with chamfered ribs springing from three octagonal central columns and slender colonettes attached to the walls. The west side has an inserted archway leading to the next-door undercroft. A probably original archway in the rear wall opens to one of a pair of rear chambers which were later barrel-vaulted in brick.

Watergates' undercroft is described in The Rows of Chester as 'the best stone vault in Chester'. The extension into No 13 Watergate Street has an inserted brick barrel vault which appears to utilise the thick sandstone walls of Nos 11 and 15 on either side. There is evidence towards the rear of the undercroft in No 15 that this too is of medieval origin although the ceiling is now spanned by massive 17th-century beams.

St Nicholas's Chapel
St Werburgh Street/Northgate Street

The former chapel of St Nicholas, just across the road from the south-west corner of the Cathedral, has probably had the most varied career of any building in Chester. It is believed to have been built early in the 14th century for Simon de Albo, Benedictine abbot of St Werburgh.

When rebuilding of the Cathedral nave began in the mid 14th century, the parishioners who worshipped in the south aisle at an altar dedicated to St Oswald transferred to the nearby chapel of St Nicholas. The surviving medieval fabric of the chapel, comprising red sandstone walls, buttresses, and window arches, is best seen from the lane at the side (Music Hall Passage).

Ownership was conveyed to the Mayor and Corporation in 1488, whereupon the former chapel was substantially altered and enlarged. Between 1545 and 1698 the building was used by the City Assembly as the Common Hall, succeeding the original meeting place (or Moot Hall) in Commonhall Street, and preceding the Exchange half-way up Northgate Street. It was then used as the Wool Hall before becoming a playhouse in 1727. Fifty years later, large parts of the building were reconstructed, first as the New Theatre, and then as the Theatre Royal. All the famous actors of the day played here and were frequently mobbed by the admiring crowds.

In 1854-5 James Harrison, a prominent local architect of the mid 19th century, adapted the building as a music hall and designed the Tudor gothic façade to St Werburgh Street. In the 20th century it was further adapted into a cinema and eventually into a shop.

The size and height of St Nicholas's Chapel is hard to appreciate and the Northgate Street elevation has been enclosed several times, most recently in the early 1990s with a stylish modern stone façade by the Biggins Sargent Partnership.

400

1000

1200

*

•
1500

1700

•
1800

•

1900

○

•
2000

WATER TOWER AND SPUR WALL
CITY WALLS

The Water Tower and the spur wall to it from Bonewaldesthorne's Tower are the only significant defensive features to survive on the City Walls. The round red sandstone tower was built at Chester's expense to protect the town from ship-borne attack via the harbour, whose waters lapped the Wall at this point. It was designed as a strongpoint from which archers could slay attackers from their rear as they attempted to assault the Walls. A similar principle of defence had been skilfully used by the designers of Edward I's castles - most locally at Flint.

In practice, however, the Water Tower (or 'New Tower' as it was originally called) had a much more peaceful role in Chester's maritime history. It was

KM

probably used to monitor shipping into and out of the Port of Chester, as a base from which to collect tolls on vessels and merchandise, and as a deterrent to pirates and Welsh raiders. That said, the Water Tower was fiercely attacked during the siege of Chester (1644-6) and the marks made by musket balls can still be seen.

The River Dee has, of course, receded over the centuries and the land around the Water Tower has gradually been reclaimed from the marshes. In 1838 the Water Tower became a small museum and a camera obscura was erected on the roof of Bonewaldesthorne's Tower. Extensive conservation work was carried out on the Water Tower and spur wall in the late 1970s and early 1980s. It is rarely open to the public nowadays, although hopes remain that it might eventually become a museum of Chester's maritime history.

SL

400
1000
1200
*
1500
1700
1800
O
1900
2000

SHUTTLEWORTHS' CRYPT
36 BRIDGE STREET

This building includes an early 14th-century undercroft spanned by two wide-span pointed sandstone arches and a number of oak beams, one of which is of massive dimensions. Two bays of the ceiling have broad oak joists of early type. The present floor has been inserted, reducing the depth of the undercroft and bringing the ceiling closer to eye level.

Like many others in Chester's central streets, this building was originally a town house above an undercroft. The upper stories were much altered and rebuilt in the 16th century and, again, in the 1760s. Construction is therefore a mixture of

sandstone, timber framing, and brown brick in Flemish bond, with the newer materials at the higher levels. Although the present-day shop fronts have no architectural value there is an interesting five-board studded door at Row level which probably dates from the 16th century.

400

1000

1200

*

1500

1700

1800

1900

2000

400

1000

1200

*

1500

38-42 WATERGATE STREET

These apparently separate buildings conceal the structure of a great medieval stone house 17.5m (57ft) wide running parallel to the Row behind undistinguished 19th and 20th-century façades. A restaurant now occupies the impressive eastern bay of the undercroft, spanned by two massive arch-braced beams and a chamfered stone arch. At Row level and above, the same cafe-restaurant occupies the former great hall and the small front chambers which were once the office and shops of medieval merchants.

The front and rear doorways near the west end of the great hall mark the former through-passage which screened the hall from the buttery which lay beyond the three archways in the party wall and which is now 'The Art Shop' (No 38 Watergate Row - the Row numbering being different from that at street level). The archways have since been blocked but can still be seen clearly inside the shop.

In the late 16th century the lofty and, no doubt, draughty great hall was sub-divided into four heated rooms. A central chimney with back-to-back inglenook fireplaces was inserted, together with a dividing wall and an intermediate cross-beam floor. The original size of the great hall is now difficult to appreciate, although exploration of the

1700

1800

1900

2000

restaurant at Row level reveals several of the original features as well as the remains of two Jacobean staircases.

It might be unfair to single this out as the most interesting building in Chester, but it is certainly a strong contender. Rarely has the medieval fabric survived so intact as in the upper levels above these undercrofts. Rarely too have any of our standing buildings been so thoroughly investigated. This was one of a group of buildings in Watergate Street which comprised the pilot study for 'The Rows Research Project'. Survey work started in 1984 and has recently culminated in a superb publication - *The Rows of Chester* - which describes the Row buildings, past and present, in all of our main streets.

Cut-away reconstruction of 38-42 Watergate Street (Painting by Graham Holme courtesy of The Chester Rows Research Project)

400

1000

1200

*

1500

1700

1800

1900

2000

400

1000

1200

*

1500

1700

1800

1900

2000

St Peter's Church
The Cross

This church stands at the centre of the walled city on the site of the Roman legionary headquarters - the principia. Although surrounded by secular buildings, it remains an important landmark from Bridge Street.

Aethelflaed, daughter of King Alfred the Great, founded the church in AD 907, but its

complete rebuilding was undertaken in the mid 14th century. Stone steps lead up to the porch, for the floor is at Row level - the builders who added the north aisle in the 15th century buried a former undercroft beneath its floor. Almost square in plan, the church has four aisles to the nave and chancel. The added 15th-century arcade is Perpendicular with carved bosses and spandrels to its arched roof trusses. The rib-vaulted baptistry under the tower has a damaged medieval fresco around a niche in the north-west pier.

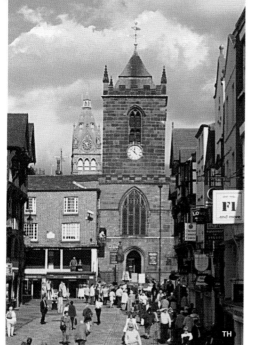

The church spire was removed c1780 after having been struck by lightning, and was replaced by a low, two-tiered pyramidal roof in the restoration carried out by John Douglas in1886. The south wall of the church, refaced by Thomas Harrison in 1804, was also altered in 1886. Douglas retained the north and south galleries within the church but added the row of square-headed windows below the main south-facing windows to bring more light into the building.

St Peter's is now an ecumenical church, and is open daily for prayer and contemplation as well as for tea and cakes.

ST MARY-ON-THE-HILL
ST MARY'S HILL

400

1000

Also called St Mary's Church or, nowadays, St Mary's Centre. This church was commissioned c1350, partly to serve the growing needs of the garrison and staff of Chester Castle. It is now an educational centre but remains consecrated. Its earliest features are the tower and chancel arches.

The south-east chapel dates from c1443 and the nave arcades, clerestory, and fine panelled oak roof are c1500. A notable 17th-century tomb has effigies of Thomas Gamul and his wife attended by their children, and monuments commemorate the Randle Holmes family of heraldic painters. The churchyard overlooks the Dee from a sandstone bluff set beautifully between Castle Square and the stone steps on St Mary's Hill.

St Mary's, like most other medieval parish churches in Chester, underwent a Victorian 'makeover'. The architect responsible for much of the work in the 1850s and 1860s was James Harrison, son of a local stonemason but no relation of Thomas Harrison, his illustrious namesake who rebuilt Chester Castle. James tackled St Mary's in 1861-2. Much of the external sandstone masonry was renewed and the tower was raised by over 9 m (30 ft) - although the tops of the pinnacles have since been removed. Further restoration followed in 1890-2 at the hands of John Pollard Seddon, whose work included rebuilding the north porch at the expense of Cheshire Freemasons.

St Mary's temporarily lost its parish church status when St Mary-Without-the-Walls was built in Handbridge in 1887. Four years later it took over from St Bridget's (hence the further restoration?) before the latter was demolished - for the second time. Conversion to St Mary's Centre followed redundancy as a parish church in 1972. In 2000, with educational activities having ceased, the future of the building is again uncertain.

1200

*

1500

1700

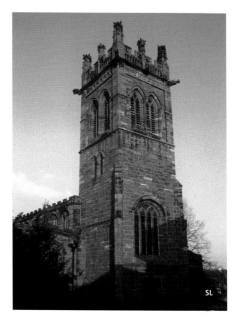

1800

•

○
1900

○
2000

400

1000

1200

*

1500

1700

1800

1900

2000

1363 • Listed Grade II*

ANCHORITE'S CELL
THE GROVES (NORTH)

Also called the 'The Hermitage', this little sandstone building which dates from the mid 14th century was a religious retreat for a reclusive monk or hermit. It is best seen from the secluded green just south of the Church of St John the Baptist, to whose collegiate precinct it belonged until the Reformation. The former cell stands on a sheer sandstone bluff overlooking a former quarry, which is now reclaimed as a riverside bowling green. The medieval building was restored as a house in the 19th century. Its entrance, on the north side, is a former church porch which was brought from St Martin's Church when it was demolished in 1897. The building was refurbished as a cottage c1970.

Bookland's Crypt

12 Bridge Street

From the front part of the bookshop six steps lead down through a mid 19th-century gothic revival stone screen to a 14th-century stone undercroft of six rib-vaulted bays. The fifth bay has a very unusual doorway leading to stairs within the thickness of the party wall, which rise to the Row floor above. This is also the only undercroft in Chester where the lie of the land allowed a window to be placed in the rear wall.

Five stone-vaulted undercrofts have survived in Chester's Rows buildings - the others being at No 28 Eastgate Street (Browns Crypt), No 11 Watergate Street (Watergates' Wine Bar) and Nos 21 and 37 Watergate Street. There are also lesser stone vaults over small spaces at the rear of a sixth undercroft. Although these are only a small proportion of the total number of medieval undercrofts in Chester, they provide evidence of some very prestigious town houses, as well as an early appreciation of the commercial benefits of fireproof warehouses.

The timber-framed building which is now at and above Row level dates from the 17th century. Known as Cowper House, it was the home of Thomas Cowper, Mayor of Chester 1641-2 and a prominent Royalist of the Civil War period. The inscription 'TC 1664' on the main façade is evidence of the repairs and improvements carried out on many of the buildings that were damaged during the hostilities.

400

1000

1200

*

1500

1700

1800

•

1900

O

2000

LECHE HOUSE

17 WATERGATE STREET (12 WATERGATE ROW)

This building, now a sofa showroom, is the best preserved and most easily understood medieval town house in the Rows. It dates from the late 14th century, was partly rebuilt in the late 15th century, and extended and improved in the 17th and 18th centuries. The ashlar undercroft retains a pair of ancient studded loading doors to the left of the shopfront. At Row level and above, the timber frame was rebuilt c1475. The hall, open to the roof, retains an original fireplace and a 17th-century overmantel with Sir John Leche's coat of arms. The central roof-truss has a large Jacobean chandelier pendant. A west gallery leads to the front chamber above the Row walk and to a substantial rear chamber above the parlour which faces a small courtyard.

Leche House, like several of its contemporaries in Watergate Street, was studied in the first phase of the Rows Research Project. The need for a thorough survey of the buildings in Chester's four main streets was highlighted in 1958, but only piecemeal and reactive work was carried out in the '60s and '70s. Then, in 1984, the Chester Archaeological Society organised a one-day conference which drew attention to the continuing uncertainty about the origin of the Rows and inspired the City and County Councils to begin the research project. Funds for a pilot study were provided by the two local authorities and The Chester Civic Trust. The results of this study stimulated interest in the project, enabling a survey of all the Row buildings to be undertaken. An interdisciplinary approach was adopted from the outset, combining the results of archaeological investigations and historical research with an appreciation of the architectural and social influences that inspired the construction and modification of these unique 'two-tier' buildings.

In the latter stages of the project, which lasted over 10 years, funds were drawn from several other sources including the Royal Commission on the Historical Monuments of England, the British Archaeological Research Trust and English Heritage. The culmination of this work (but not necessarily the end of the story) is *The Rows of Chester* published by English Heritage in 1999 and launched at a reception organised by Chester Civic Trust.

Cut-away reconstruction of Leche House on the south side of Watergate Street (Painting by Graham Holme, courtesy of The Chester Rows Research Project)

400

1000

1200

*

1500

1700

1800

1900

2000

THE OLD DEE BRIDGE

HANDBRIDGE

This bridge is one of Chester's major monuments. It stands near the site of a Roman bridge across the Dee and replaced earlier timber bridges which had served Chester for more than three hundred years. The present sandstone bridge has seven arches of varied profile. The two arches nearest to the north bank span the leat dammed by the weir which used to power the Mills of Dee. The piers between the arches have pointed stone cutwaters to protect the masonry from the force of floodwaters and spring tides. The sixth arch has the longest span, beyond which the massive pier has a rectangular projection upstream which was the base of a defensive gatehouse. The short stone arch between this and the Handbridge bank replaces the medieval drawbridge. The gatehouse was demolished in 1781 and the footway on the upstream (east) side of the bridge was widened in 1826.

An engineering inspection of the bridge in 1999 provided a rare opportunity for archaeologists to examine the material beneath the modern road surface. Trial pits were excavated in several positions

JMP

400

1000

1200

*

1500

1700

•
1800

•

1900

O
2000

400

1000

1200

*

1500

1700

1800

1900

O
2000

above the arches and bridge piers. In arch 7 (closest to the Handbridge bank) there was a great depth of demolition rubble, mortar, sandstone, ashlar blocks, and bricks. This fill material is believed to be evidence of a major repair which may have coincided with the demolition of the gatehouse. Another pit revealed a Liverpool halfpenny token of 1791-4 and pottery of a similar date. Excavation above arch 5 seems to have been the most rewarding. At a depth of about 1 m (3 ft) below the present road surface the archaeologists discovered a substantial surface of river cobbles embedded in a layer of soft sand - could this be the original medieval road surface?

400

1000

1200

*

1500

1700

1800

1900

●
○
2000

THE BLUE BELL

63-65 NORTHGATE STREET

The Blue Bell is part of a small group of buildings known as Lorimer's Row. Although they are not, and never have been, Row buildings of the more usual pattern, the upper floors are built over the pavement to form a covered arcade. A uniquely surviving feature is the detached sales booth which stands at the front of No 65, between the pavement and the road.

The two town houses of sandstone, timber framing, and brick are now joined together by the stair to their upper floors. They stand within the City Walls, some 300 metres north of the Rows, but are more modest in size than the central medieval houses. No 63, the southern house, is some fifty years older than its neighbour. Both houses had an upper floor inserted in their formerly full-height halls. The restaurant upstairs in No 63 is open to the roof and has a fine crownpost truss, a rare feature in Cheshire.

The Blue Bell was an inn and tavern for most of its life; the first recorded licence was issued in 1494. It was threatened by a road improvement scheme in the early 1930s, closed in 1936, and re-opened in 1948 as an antiques shop. By the late 1950s, it was in such a bad state of repair that it was again threatened with demolition. A campaign involving the newly-formed Chester Civic Trust succeeded in rescuing the building in 1960. After restoration, it was re-opened as a shop and then became a restaurant in 1984.

THE BOOT INN

17 EASTGATE STREET & 9 EASTGATE ROW

One of Chester's oldest surviving public houses is the Boot Inn, which is at Row level on the north side of Eastgate Street. Evidence of the date of this former merchant's house is difficult to find, but coursed medieval sandstone masonry could be seen in the undercroft, now divided between the shop and its stockroom (No 17 Eastgate Street) and the

beer cellar of the inn (No 9 Eastgate Row). The stone party wall can also be seen in the rear yard of the inn.

The timber-framed building at Row level and above dates from the early to mid 17th century - possibly commensurate with the opening of the inn in 1643. The façade of the Boot was rebuilt and restored in the late 19th century but the structure is otherwise intact, with a wattle-and-daub panel on display inside the present entrance. Until 1988 most of the front section at Row level was a barber's shop. Anecdotal evidence suggests that a landlord in the 19th century was also a barber. Prior to this, there was allegedly a brothel on the premises (how convenient if all three had been there at once!). In any case, prior to the 1988 restoration, the inn was tucked away at the back of the building and was reached via a corridor alongside the barber's shop. Above this and the Row walkway is a fine 17th-century oak-panelled parlour which extends 7.6 m (25 ft) back from the street frontage and is one of the largest surviving from that period.

The Boot Inn was carefully restored and enlarged by Samuel Smith's Brewery in 1988.

400

1000

1200

*
1500

1700

1800

1900

2000

PLAN OF CHESTER IN 1581
(EXTRACT FROM PLAN BY BRAUN AND HOGENBERG)

CHAPTER 7

DISSOLUTION, REVOLUTION, RESTORATION
1501 - 1700

SIMON WARD AND OLIVER BOTT

These two centuries witnessed great changes in the built heritage and included two major events: the dissolution of the monasteries (1538-40) and the Civil War (1642-6). The River Dee continued to silt and the decay of the port was only partially offset by quays downstream. In spite of wars and plagues, the population grew, resulting in both denser occupation within the built-up area and the growth of suburbs.

The early 16th century produced the last flowering of the English Gothic. The Abbey church was finally completed after two and a half centuries of building. Work is also attested at Chester's three friaries. However, change was on the way, and in 1538 the friaries were surrendered to the King, followed in 1540 by the Abbey and the Nunnery. In 1541, the Abbey was refounded as Chester Cathedral. The other religious houses passed into private ownership, although some of the buildings survived for many years.

Fashions in living accommodation were changing, with a desire for more privacy, expressed in the decline of the medieval open hall and the setting of houses in spacious grounds, eg Stanley Palace. The precincts of the dissolved friaries and nunnery allowed scope for this. Even now, the former monastic precincts tend to contain less dense development than the historic commercial core.

The City enjoyed a building boom between the Dissolution and the Civil War. New buildings were timber-framed and still incorporated the Rows. Earlier fabric was frequently retained. Subdivision of open halls resulted in several fine Jacobean staircases. Fireplaces with chimneys replaced open hearths, and these too gave opportunities for ornament. Internally, decorated plaster ceilings and externally, carved timber embellished these new buildings. As the suburbs developed, some of the more substantial citizens moved into them, eg Charles Walley, the Mayor in 1644-6, who lived at The Bars.

During the Civil War, damage was extensive. All the suburbs, as well as Handbridge and Boughton, were destroyed. Within the walls many buildings were damaged. The medieval hospitals of St Giles in Boughton and Little St John at the Northgate were lost. The mills at the bridge were put out of action. Royalist soldiers sacked the Nunnery (the Chester house of Sir William Brereton the parliamentary commander), and parliamentary ones the Bishop's Palace.

The City Walls were breached and battered. Royalist citizens suffered fines and loss of office. In consequence, the rebuilding of Chester took several decades. A number of buildings bear dates from the second half of the 17th century testifying to a period of repair and reconstruction. The later 17th century also witnessed the start of Row enclosure, the earliest being in 1643 at the town house of Sir Richard Grosvenor which is now the Falcon Inn.

Throughout this period, new building materials made few inroads. In 1671, the Corporation required all houses on the four main streets to be roofed in slate or tile. This was a measure to improve fire safety (the Great Fire of London having occurred only a few years before) and implies that many buildings were still thatched. One or two departures from tradition, such as the Earl of Shrewsbury's town house (now the Bear and Billet) of 1664, and the 'Dutch Houses', c1670, must have created a stir with their 'foreign' architectural influences but, otherwise, the radical new styles which were being adopted elsewhere in England were slow to appear in Chester. Bridge House (now the Oddfellows Hall) in Lower Bridge Street was probably the first to break the mould in 1676 with its neo-classical design. Nevertheless, with such notable exceptions, brick was little used until the end of the period, when some brick

houses were constructed, eg in Castle Street. The Exchange in Market Square was built of stone and brick in 1695-8 in the new style and several medieval town houses were transformed with handsome new brick façades, eg Gamul House and Booth Mansion, both c1700. However, many timber-framed buildings survived and continued to influence the City's architecture, for it was these buildings that formed the models for the 19th-century's 'black and white' revival which gives Chester its unique character today.

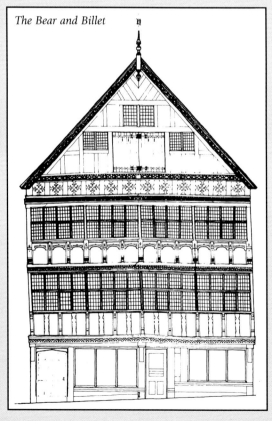

The Bear and Billet

BUILDING   PAGE

Gamul House *(c1510)*   92

Ye Olde Edgar *(c1570)*   93

Stanley Palace *(1591)*   94

Tudor House *(1603)*   95

Bishop Lloyd's Palace *(1615)*   96

Pied Bull Hotel *(c1620)*   98

13 & 14 Abbey Square *(1626)*   99

Boughton Hall *(c1630)*   100

Ye Olde Custom House Inn *(1637)*   101

The Old Rectory, Bridge Street *(c1650)*   102

The Nine Houses *(c1655)*   103

The Bear & Billet *(1664)*   104

The Dutch Houses *(c1670)*   106

Oddfellows' Hall *(1676)*   107

1

GAMUL HOUSE
52-58 LOWER BRIDGE STREET & I GAMUL TERRACE

Gamul House, basically a late medieval town house, is puzzling because of successive alterations over five centuries. The great hall, which is now a restaurant, was refronted in brick with a classical doorway and elliptical windows c1700 at the same time as the Row walk was altered. The undercroft, down steps from the street, was revaulted in brick later in the 18th century. Three small shops which project under the raised terrace were added in the 19th century, and fifteen stone steps were built to give access to the great hall at first floor level. Some of the cottages which were built in 1872 in the court behind Gamul House survive today in Gamul Place.

The most interesting external feature of Gamul House is the brick façade to the great hall, but on the inside the mouldings

to a blocked high level casement and the doorway to the solar (or private parlour) date the structure back at least to 1510. The great hall has a 17th-century plaster ceiling and a carved sandstone fireplace.

Gamul House was the home of the influential Gamul family which entertained Charles I there when he visited the besieged city in September 1645.

YE OLDE EDGAR

86 & 88 LOWER BRIDGE STREET

Ye Olde Edgar marks the revival of new building in Chester after the long hiatus which spanned the reigns of Henry VIII, Edward VI, and Mary. It was built as two houses which were later united to serve as an inn, but are now once again dwellings. Their timber-framed exterior has notable features which are characteristic of the Elizabethan era. The corner-post shows how the trunk and bough of an oak tree could be hewn to support the projecting second storey. The repaired vertical post shaped from the trunk has a branch which curves out gently to carry the projecting corner of the jetty-beams to the front and end of the building. The ground floor walls have largely been repaired in brick, but timbers of the upper storey preserve the close-studded form used during the 16th century with posts at short intervals but no intermediate rail between floor and ceiling.

The building retains the name of the former inn which was, apparently, a tribute to King Edgar of England. According to tradition, Edgar visited Chester in AD 973 and was rowed on the River Dee by eight subject kings in token of their submission to him. The inn sign, which was once fixed to the Shipgate Street side of the building, depicted this episode and was captured in one of Louise Rayner's many paintings of 19th-century Chester.

400

1000

1200

1500

*

1700

1800

1900

●

2000

400

1000

1200

1500

*

1700

1800

1900

2000

STANLEY PALACE
83 WATERGATE STREET

Stanley Palace, formerly called Derby House, stands on or near the site previously occupied by the Dominican Friars (the 'Black Friars') in medieval times. It was built for Sir Peter Warburton, a Chester lawyer and MP for the City, then passed as his daughter's dowry to the Stanleys of Alderley.

The timber-framed house is unusual in having its front at right-angles to the street. This main range is intact, but the shorter wing facing the street was reconstructed in simplified form in 1935. The house has more the character of a country house than an urban palace; long and low, it has only two storeys, framed in oak and standing on a modest sandstone plinth. The façade has four gables, of which the left three are original, designed in the Elizabethan manner with leaded mullioned-and-transomed casements, quadrant oak braces to the small plaster panels, carved figures between the windows, and wavy oak struts to the gables. The interior has a long oak-beamed hall whence a great oak stair leads to the gallery. Each storey has a good early 18th-century room west of the stair bay.

In 1866 the building was in prospect of being dismantled and transported to the USA. It was saved by the Chester Archaeological Society and in 1889 sold back to the Derby family on condition that it would be preserved. In 1928 the Earl of Derby gave Stanley Palace to Chester Corporation, shortly after which it underwent a major restoration. The building is still owned by Chester City Council and is now managed by the Friends of Stanley Palace, who open it to the public when other uses allow.

DN

TUDOR HOUSE
29 & 31 LOWER BRIDGE STREET

This house only earns its 'Tudor' name by a hairsbreadth, for it probably dates from the year of Elizabeth I's death, when James I became our first Stuart king. The plaque dated 1503 above the door is erroneous and should read 1603. The timber-framed house was extended to the rear in the mid 17th century and the front was rebuilt in 1728, when the Row walk through its second storey was enclosed. The location of the former Row and Stall (behind the three early 18th-century sash windows) can still be seen from the position of the timbers embedded in its south side. The front door has a Tudor-arched case, the third and fourth storeys are jettied forward and have leaded mullioned and transomed casements.

AVP

Originally built for a wealthy Chester merchant, Tudor House, like many of its contemporaries, has had a variety of uses in its time. The two undercrofts at street level are now united as a single shop but were once quite separate. One was a bake-house while the other was the Britannia Inn with rooms above and, apparently, in the neighbouring building (33 Lower Bridge Street) when the two were linked together by a bridge which was a continuation of the Row walkway. The ground floor premises recently became a delicatessen and café, while the two uppermost floors have been sensitively restored as a rather splendid private apartment.

400

1000

1200

1500

*

●

1700

●

1800

1900

○
○
2000

400

1000

1200

1500

*

1700

1800

1900

O

2000

BISHOP LLOYD'S PALACE
51-53 WATERGATE ROW

This house (hardly a palace!) was built for George Lloyd, Bishop of Sodor and Man from 1597 to 1605, then Bishop of Chester from 1605 to 1615. The undercrofts at street level date from the Middle Ages but the bishop's house above was to an entirely new design.

The date carved on the westernmost front gable indicates completion in 1615, the year of George Lloyd's death. There is no evidence that either he or his family took up residence, yet nearly 400 years later the building still bears his name.

In fact, this property was originally two town houses, with George Lloyd being more clearly associated with only the westernmost (No 53). The main façade,

with a pair of ornate oak-framed gables facing onto the street, reflects something of the original form but underwent a radical restoration in 1899. The Chester architect T M Lockwood rebuilt the steps from the street and much of the gable to No 51, but left the other gable largely intact. Eight carved panels between the Row beam and the window above depict the arms of James I and of Sodor and Man, plus biblical scenes. Between the window-head and the tie-beam are ten arched carved panels, and three to each side of the attic window. The pilasters to the chamber window are an attempt, early for Chester, at the classical style. Some of the brackets on the Row posts are Jacobean, carved with bearded giants, beasts, and an owl, shaped like ships' figureheads; the lighter brackets are Lockwood's carved replacements of earlier timbers.

The Row storey contains shops, now with no visible features of special interest, but the recessed porch between them leads by an oak stair to a pair of great panelled chambers, one under each gable, overlooking the street. The east chamber

has a massive but unrefined fireplace and overmantel as well as an equally ornate plaster ceiling. The over-sized fireplace has evidently been transferred from another building, but the provenance of the ceiling (which has a pattern very similar to that in St Anselm's Chapel at Chester Cathedral) is still uncertain.

The house is now the headquarters of The Chester Civic Trust, which also administers its use by other organisations or individuals for lectures, classes and social functions. Bishop Lloyd's Palace is open to the public for several hours a week and can be visited by groups by prior arrangement (details can be found next to the door at Row level).

The west chamber has another clumsily impressive fireplace whose overmantel depicts Cupid riding a lion in an arcadian setting. This, and the much more plainly decorated plaster ceiling, are believed to be original features of the building.

400

1000

1200

1500

1700

1800

1900

2000

PIED BULL HOTEL
57 NORTHGATE STREET

The Pied Bull Hotel is difficult to date precisely. It is timber-framed, but by 1660 it had been refaced in brick to King Street then, with more skill, some fifty years later, the front was remodelled to provide the attractive arcade on Northgate Street. Some timber framing visible on the first floor landing may go back to 1600 or a little earlier, but other features such as the great sandstone fireplace in the front room of the ground floor are probably early or mid 17th century. The hotel is almost certainly the inn which the eccentric traveller George Borrow described in his Wild Wales in 1870, where he admired the strapping chambermaid, commented on the ale, and strode into the porch to spit onto the street the sample of Cheshire cheese which he had been invited to taste.

Accommodation is still provided at the Pied Bull on the first and second floors, where most of the historic features can be found. The bar area on the ground floor has been opened up and modernised, sadly losing the individual rooms and much of the character in the process. Apart from the stone fireplace with its armorial painting on the overmantel and the nearby cupboards in the oak panelling; the other noteworthy feature is the 17th-century oak stairway. Carved faces to the closed strings, shaped newels and pierced balusters are still visible on the open-well stair which once extended to the full height of the building.

13 AND 14 ABBEY SQUARE

These are a pair of modest sandstone cottages typical of those built in Cheshire during the 17th century. The main roof is parallel with Abbey Square, but each cottage has a front gable and No 13 has an added porch. The cottages were built by Bishop Bridgeman to house lay clerks (or 'vicars choral') to the Cathedral.

Abbey Square originated as the courtyard of the Benedictine abbey which contained its secular buildings such as the bakery and brewhouse - Henry VIII had reconstituted the abbey as a cathedral in 1540 when its former abbot became its first dean. Six cottages are said to have been built in 1626 on the site of the abbey's kitchen - the masonry probably having been salvaged from the demolished buildings. Only these two have survived and, with the exception of the Abbey Gateway (*qv*), they are the oldest buildings around the courtyard. Although by no means 'medieval', the cottages are a reminder of how the abbey precinct would have looked before it was transformed in the 18th century to house the Cathedral's dean, chapter and other office-holders.

JLW

400

1000

1200

1500

*

1700

1800

1900

2000

BOUGHTON HALL
CHAPEL LANE

Originally a country house, Boughton Hall was later a children's home and is now in use as offices. It is the oldest property in the Boughton suburb of Chester and dates back to the early part of the 17th century. A fireplace in the hall bears the date 1655, but this may have been added when the house was rebuilt after its destruction by fire in 1643 during the early stages of the Civil War. In July of that year, Parliamentary forces made their first attack on Chester by raiding the extensive outworks to the east of the city. As a precaution, the citizens razed Boughton to the ground, and in the battles that followed little survived of the suburbs of Christleton, Spital, Flookersbrook, or Boughton.

It is thought that the original house on this site was built before 1579. When it was rebuilt, it had the contemporary 'E'-shaped plan with the three short wings of the main façade facing west. The recess to the left of the centre wing and entrance porch is believed to have been filled in c1800. Such of the 17th -century building as is still visible between the later additions is of brown bricks worked into simple and robust details at the corners and along the eaves. As seen today, the house is largely Georgian, having undergone many alterations and extensions during the 18th century, and many fine fittings and furnishings of this period still survive inside. Another wing was added in the 19th century, and the house was further altered in the 20th century.

YE OLDE CUSTOM HOUSE INN

69 & 71 WATERGATE STREET

Two former houses with their undercrofts (now beer cellars) were combined to form the inn. The east house (No 69) is dated 1637 but the west house (No 71) is probably early 18th century. The former Row walk at the level of the licensed rooms was enclosed in 1711. The rear wing of the inn, facing Weaver Street, was formerly a modest cottage built on the burgage plot behind No 69.

The much-restored timber-framed gable facing onto Watergate Street bears the initials T&AW which are believed to be those of Thomas and Ann Weaver. Conversion from town house to inn probably occurred at the time when the Row was enclosed, but could have been earlier. Then known as The Star Inn, its name was changed in the late 18th century because the custom house of the Port of Chester was just across the road.

In contrast to its older neighbour, the façade of No 71 is of irregularly bonded brickwork with sash windows to second and third storeys. Internally, both buildings have been altered, most recently in the early 1990s when an extension was added to the rear of No 71. Despite this, some parts of Ye Olde Custom House Inn manage to retain the character of a traditional public house with rooms of domestic size served from a central bar. There are some oak beams c1642 and a carved stone fireplace with a classical surround of painted wood.

400

1000

1200

1500

*

1700

*
●

1800

1900

O

●
2000

THE OLD RECTORY

43 BRIDGE STREET & 49 BRIDGE STREET ROW

This diminutive building replaces an earlier undercroft and town house. In 1659 the then almost new house was bequeathed to St Michael's Parish for use as its rectory. A modern shopfront at street level covers the undercroft structure and the interior is largely lined, but the timber-framed front of the Row and upper storeys is intact. Oak corner posts rise from the Row floor to the eaves; the ceiling beam and joists of the Row are visible, but the shop front dates from the early 20th century. The plaster panels of the third and fourth storeys are ornately shaped and the timbers carved with patterns - it is a good façade, now squeezed between younger and heavier neighbours.

Most of the interior, now a greetings card shop, is accessible to would-be customers. Visible 17th-century features include the front wall, a fine but now incomplete moulded plaster ceiling, and the form of the galleried great hall, open to the roof. The frame of the original rear wall crosses the shop at the foot of the good 18th-century stair which rises to the enlarged third storey. Looking towards the front from the stair, one can see four panels below the stairwell rail which depict the Stations of the Cross in a late medieval manner. In fact they are plaster panels painted to mimic wood, installed by an antique dealer named Crawford who, upon closure of the rectory in 1907, converted the building into a shop.

1000

1200

1500

*
1700

o

1800

1900
•

2000

c1655 • Listed Grade II

THE NINE HOUSES
6 TO 16 (EVEN NUMBERS) PARK STREET

These houses, of which only six survive, are the only remaining pre-19th-century almshouses in Chester. The front of the cottages facing the City Wall is a mixture of masonry, timber-framing, and infill brickwork. The bottom storey is constructed in brick upon a low sandstone plinth, with oak-boarded doors in stone-dressed openings. The timber-framed

SL

upper storey is jettied over the lower structure and has a projecting dormer gable to each cottage. This combination is unusual in Chester - where the ground floors of old buildings beyond the Rows tend to have timber-framing directly onto sandstone plinths.

The almshouses were rescued from collapse and renovated by the City Council in 1968-9, after campaigns to save them led by The Chester Civic Trust and the Chester Archaeological Society. A conservation report was prepared by the Society for the Protection of Ancient Buildings (SPAB), but parts of the structure were so decayed that the end wall was repaired in old brick and the whole of the back wall was rebuilt anew.

DN

400

1000

1200

1500

* 1700

1800

1900

2000

THE BEAR AND BILLET
94 LOWER BRIDGE STREET

The Bear and Billet was orginally the Earl of Shrewsbury's residence in Chester, perhaps the last of the oak-framed town houses to be built here. In time it became an inn which took its name from the Earl's heraldic device, a bear and the billet or stake to which it was shackled. Now a restaurant with a ground-floor bar, it has been renamed Benson's at the Billet.

The fine oak-framed façade is almost intact, but changes of use since it ceased to be a peer's residence have brought alterations to the interior. Evidently the Earl of Shrewsbury sought to be a merchant, for he chose his site at what was then the head of the tidal port. His house has parallels with those built at a similar time along Amsterdam's canals. The three main storeys were domestic but the loft in the roof was designed to serve as a small warehouse with a broad pair of boarded doors, above which is the replaced bracket for a hoist to raise and lower merchandise. The plan and form of the house spring from the late Middle Ages, but details such as the console-shaped brackets which support the jettied cross-beams of the façade were early attempts at

neo-classicism. The mullioned windows to each storey stretch uninterrupted from side to side of the building, so make it, like the famous Hardwick Hall built a hundred years earlier, 'more glass than wall'. Although altered, the bar and restaurant display much of the authentic timber frame.

400

1000

1200

1500

* 1700

1800

1900

2000

THE DUTCH HOUSES
20, 22 AND 24 BRIDGE STREET ROW

400

1000

1200

1500

1700

1800

1900

2000

The revivial of economic activity which followed the restoration of the monarchy in 1660 soon had an impact on Chester's war-damaged townscape. Maritime trade with Ireland, Spain, Portugal, and the Low Countries may have influenced the design of some of the more ambitious schemes of the day. If the Bear and Billet (*qv*) is reminiscent of merchants' houses in Amsterdam, it is not too surprising to see similar architectural styles emerging elsewhere in Chester. The building we now know as the 'Dutch Houses' was erected c1670 above earlier undercrofts. Standing four storeys high and three bays wide, this was probably the tallest and most impressive building in Bridge Street for over 200 years.

The Dutch Houses were rescued from disuse and advanced decay in 1973-5 by Chester City Council. The whole façade was taken down and rebuilt, and much of the structural timberwork was replaced by steel, but this early instance of post-war restoration involved the loss of many internal features of interest and questionable alterations to the exterior. To Chester's benefit, the renovation has preserved the form of a key building at the corner of Bridge Street and Commonhall Street, secured the restoration of a good moulded plaster ceiling in the third storey chamber of No 24, and encouraged the rapid improvement of techniques for the survey and conservation of historic buildings. The unusual form and details of the building may have earned it the name Dutch Houses. The gabled attic, elsewhere jettied forward, is set back from the lower storeys, the third and fourth storeys are decorated with barley-sugar shaped pilasters, and the walls are rendered.

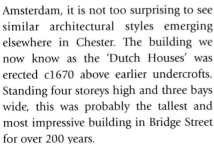

ODDFELLOWS' HALL (BRIDGE HOUSE)

16-24 LOWER BRIDGE STREET

JLW

In stark contrast to buildings such as the Bear and Billet (*qv*) and Bookland (*qv*), which were, respectively, built and remodelled in 1664, The Oddfellows' Hall - or Bridge House as it is more properly called - marks a radical departure from Chester's half-timber tradition. It is surprising to see that only twelve years separate these buildings, but important to realise that by the 1670s the unfashionable Rows were starting to disappear from outlying areas such as Lower Bridge Street. Bridge House was an example of this.

Lady Mary Calveley petitioned the City Assembly for permission to demolish her Row property and replace it with something 'as may be a grace and ornament to the City'. She was fined the substantial sum of £20 for the loss of the Row but was, nevertheless, permitted to build her fine new mansion. It was the first house in central Chester to be designed in a correct neo-classical manner, with pilasters and a bold baroque cornice to the front. The original symmetrical frontage of five bays had two quadrant stone stairs leading via a stone landing to the central entrance at first floor level, but during the 19th century the ground floor was extended forward to accommodate three shops, when a street-level entrance to the house was formed and a sixth bay was added to the north.

MP

Now the Oddfellows' Hall, the fine, richly ornamented baroque interior is private. The dating of the house to the late 17th century results from research undertaken in 1990 and is a few years earlier than that given on the blue plaque attached to the front.

400

1000

1200

1500

*
1700

1800

1900

2000

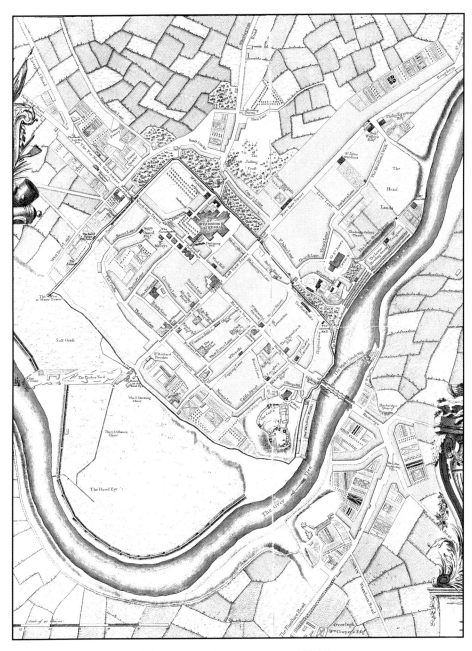

PLAN OF CHESTER IN 1745
(EXTRACT FROM PLAN BY ALEXANDER DE LAVAUX)

CHAPTER 8

GEORGIAN DECORUM
1701 - 1800

DEREK NUTTALL AND STEPHEN LANGTREE

The 18th century was a period of great significance in the development of Chester. At the start, the city was little bigger than it had been a hundred years earlier, but by the end it was spreading outwards and large areas within the City Walls had been either built upon for the first time or substantially remodelled. Building materials changed, new architectural styles were adopted, and Chester was transformed - but, thankfully, not beyond all recognition! It would be misleading, however, to suggest that this was a gradual and seamless process. The first half of the 18th century, up to about 1755, was a period of stability but relatively slow growth. New buildings were modest in number but not necessarily in size or style, eg the Blue Coat School, Park House, Dee House, and the 'Old Bishop's Palace'. From the 1750s onwards things changed more quickly. Commissioned projects, usually for individual town houses, were overtaken by wholesale redevelopments such as Abbey Square, and speculations such as Stanley Place and Nicholas Street. Previously open land within the Walls soon filled with housing, and Chester became a 'fashionable' city.

To some, the term 'Georgian Architecture' epitomises the 18th century, although strictly speaking this applies only to the reigns of the four Georges, starting with the accession of George I in 1714 and ending with the death of George IV in 1830. The transition from vernacular styles to the more prescriptive use of brick, stone, and slate had, in fact, already begun in the preceding reigns of Charles II, James II, William III, and Queen Anne (collectively, 1660-1714). Timber-framed buildings were no longer acceptable. Their replacement by the more durable brick and stone was an outcome of the Great Fire of London

The Albion Hotel (now Park House)

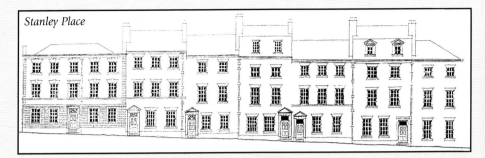

Stanley Place

(1666), following which the devastated capital was rebuilt in fire-resistant materials. The use of brick, slate, and stone was also facilitated by the improvement of roads following the Turnpike Act of 1706, and later still by the opening of canals which enabled building materials to be transported over large distances at low cost.

Like most towns in England, Chester has a large number of buildings which, from their classical, symmetrical appearance, and the use of brick and stone, are generally described as 'Georgian'. Many were, indeed, constructed during the 18th century, but a great number of these 'Georgian' buildings conceal much older structures, having had brick façades applied to timber-framed buildings. These can be seen mainly fronting the four main streets of Chester.

Of the true 18th-century buildings, one of the first in Chester to employ the new style and materials was Shipgate House, off Lower Bridge Street. The bricks used in Georgian buildings were often made locally and varied in size, becoming larger and more uniform as the century progressed. For much of the period, the Flemish bond was the usual method of bricklaying, with stone used for window and door lintels and for the quoins at the corners of buildings. By the last quarter of the century, new buildings attained considerable heights, often of three storeys together with a half-cellar (the 'ground floor' was reached by a short flight of steps). A particularly fine example of a late 18th-century terrace can be seen on the west side of Nicholas Street, while the buildings on three sides of Abbey Square and in Abbey Street which, surprisingly, date from the 1720s through to the 1820s, are fine examples of true Georgian houses.

During the 18th century, three of Chester's ancient gates were rebuilt as arches. These were the Eastgate, the Watergate, and the Bridgegate. All built of stone, they epitomise the classical architecture which was increasingly in vogue from the 1760s onwards. Other, non-domestic, buildings of the end of this century include the locks, basins, and warehouses on the Chester Canal, and significant parts of Chester Castle, the rebuilding of which was started in 1788 but not completed until well into the 19th century.

When compared with other parts of the country, Chester seemed slow to embrace the new materials and styles at the end of the 17th century, but by the end of the 18th century it was an altogether different story.

Building

Page

Park House *(1715-17)* 112

Shipgate House *(Early 18th century)* 113

Blue Coat School *(1717)* 114

Boughton Lodge *(Early 18th century)* 116

Dee House *(c1730, Chapel added 1869)* 117

Old Bishop's Palace *(1740s)* 118

St John's Rectory *(c1750)* 119

Abbey Square *(1754-61 and 1820s)* 120

Abbey Street *(1760s and 1820s)* 122

Chester Royal Infirmary *(1758-61)* 123

Bridge Place *(c1760 onward)* 124

Chester Canal *(1772-79)* 125

Canal Cutting *(1772-79)* 126

Northgate Locks *(1772-79, modified 1790s)* 127

King Street *(King's Buildings 1775-76)* 128

Forest House *(1770s/80s)* 129

Sedan House, Stanley Place *(c1780)* 130

Nicholas Street *(1780-81)* 131

The Bridgegate *(1782)* 132

The Watergate *(1788)* 133

Chester Castle *(1788-1812)* 134

Telford's Warehouse *(1790s)* 136

Leadworks' Shot Tower *(1800)* 137

1

400

1000

1200

1500

1700

1800

1900

2000

PARK HOUSE
37 TO 41 LOWER BRIDGE STREET

An imposing Georgian middle-class town house, built c1717 for Elizabeth Booth. Construction is in red brick, rendered to the street frontage, with a Tuscan porch approached by steps. The property was extended in the late 18th century and was subsequently the Albion Hotel, then the Talbot Hotel. The large central hall has been used as a ballroom, an assembly room, and an antiques emporium. The basement is now a wine bar and the remainder of the building is used as offices.

When converted from a private mansion to the Albion Hotel in 1818, the two acres of parkland behind the house became Chester's first public pleasure gardens. They stretched back to the City Wall at Park Street, incorporating extensive flower gardens and a bowling green. Both fashionable and extremely popular, the hotel and its gardens were praised by Hugh Roberts in his Chester Guide of 1851, and by Hemingway in his History of the City of Chester.

The grounds closed in 1865 (as Grosvenor Park was being laid out) and the land was developed with working-class terraced houses, such as Albion Street (qv).

SHIPGATE HOUSE
2 SHIPGATE STREET

Probably deriving its name from the old Shipgate, an archway through the City Walls, originally to the west of the present Bridgegate (and now rebuilt in Grosvenor Park), this is one of the town houses which may date from the 17th century but is essentially of early 18th-century construction.

The basement has coursed sandstone external walls which have been described as 'medieval' but are probably early 17th century. Six chamfered oak cross-beams span part of the basement, above which some late 17th-century elements survive at the rear of the house. The frontage is believed to have been rebuilt around the middle of the 18th century and is of Flemish bond red-brown brickwork and finely carved stone dressings. An architectural feature is the overhanging eaves of the grey slate hipped roof.

Over the basement are three storeys, with the front door approached by an L-shaped stone staircase of five and four steps on brick supports. Inside, the ground floor is linked to the upper storeys by a fine open-well oak stair with square newels and having two barleysugar balusters per step. This staircase continues up to the third storey and attic.

AVP

Shipgate House and the adjacent cottage were purchased by Cheshire County Council in 1963. The intention was to demolish these, and other nearby buildings, to make way for an extension of County Hall. However, the plan was fiercely resisted by Chester Civic Trust whose chairman, Dr Quentin Hughes, put forward a conservation scheme for Shipgate Street. The Trust eventually prevailed and, once the City Council's conservation programme for the Bridgegate area got underway, Shipgate House was substantially restored between 1971 and 1974. The construction of new houses in Shipgate Street (*qv*) and St Mary's Hill followed in the 1980s.

400

1000

1200

1500

1700

*

1800

1900

2000

1717 • Listed Grade II*

BLUE COAT SCHOOL
UPPER NORTHGATE STREET

This building, now used by the History Department of Chester College of Higher Education, dates from 1717, though with later additions. Its origins lie in a medieval hospital which occupied the site until demolition prior to the siege of Chester, and to the foundation in 1700 of a charity school for poor boys of the city. This was the first school to be established outside London under the auspices of the Society for Promoting Christian Knowledge (SPCK). Although this school was first set up in the cathedral precincts, purpose-built premises were erected on the old hospital site seventeen years later; almshouses were provided at the back, as successors to the medieval hospital.

TH

SL

The original building was L-shaped, with a south wing (adjacent to the City Walls) housing a chapel and the main section at right angles to it embracing a schoolroom, dormitories, and other accommodation. A north wing was added in 1733, so that the building occupied three sides of the courtyard. In 1854 the central section was enlarged by the construction of a new façade

closer to Northgate Street. It was then that the statue of the Blue Coat boy - modelled on one of the pupils at the time - was inserted over the central passageway and the present almshouses were built to replace those of the 18th century. The clock dates to 1855. An interpretative plaque in Northgate Street, overlooking the canal, shows the Blue Coat School before these 19th-century alterations.

The school continued until 1949, but the Blue Coat Trustees continue to administer the endowments, mainly to assist the work of the church schools in Chester.

The ornamental iron railings and gates along the Northgate Street frontage were reinstated in 1987 under an environmental improvement project organised by Chester Civic Trust.

400

1000

1200

1500

1700

1800

1900

2000

BOUGHTON LODGE
58 AND 60 FILKINS LANE, GT BOUGHTON

This house and cottage (now converted into a house, flats and cottage) has traces of a late 16th-century or 17th-century building on the site but, as in all the eastern suburbs, properties were razed to the ground in the 1640s to deprive the advancing Parliamentary forces of any shelter.

Boughton Hall (*qv*), which was itself destroyed by fire in 1643, is the oldest house in the area. The next oldest is a small group of properties around Chapel Lane comprising Boughton Lodge, Boughton Grange, and the Manor House, all dating from the 18th century. An Ordnance Survey map of 1875 shows that all these houses had very large gardens and orchards - the latter being a feature of the area which is still recalled in the name of a nearby public house, 'The Cherry Orchard'.

Cecil Wright's History of the Civil Parish of Great Boughton (1997) throws more light on the area with the explanation that Chapel Lane (part of which has since been added to Filkins Lane) derives its name from the chapel which stood on the site of Boughton Lodge.

The present building has three storeys beneath grey slate roofs. The walls are rendered and painted. Evidence of a timber frame is suggested, but the most visible features are the Gothic-style doorway and windows which presumably date from the mid 19th century.

DEE HOUSE

LITTLE ST JOHN STREET

Grade II-listed, but currently unoccupied and badly dilapidated, Dee House has achieved more notoriety for what once lay beneath it than for the building itself.

LM

The core of Dee House (five bays wide and three storeys high, with a centrally positioned doorway) was built c1730 as a town house for James Comberbach, a wealthy merchant and Mayor of Chester in 1727-8. Extensions to the south and south-west were made in the 1740s, resulting in an L-shape plan. Dee House remained a private residence, owned by the Comberbach family, until it was sold to the Anglican Church c1850.

In 1854 Dee House was acquired by the Faithful Companions of Jesus, who established a convent school and commissioned construction of the east wing including a chapel on the ground floor. Designed in contrasting Gothic Revival style by the Liverpool architect Edmund Kirby, the chapel was built between 1867-9. The west wing was rebuilt c1900 (four bays wide and three storeys high) in a neo-Georgian style to match the core block. The Ursulines of Crewe took over the school in 1925 and in 1929 added a new block to the south, the construction of which led to the discovery of the Roman amphitheatre. The convent closed in the early 1970s and the buildings were used by British Telecom until the early 1990s since when they have been empty.

Due to its varied uses, the original building has seen several alterations from the middle of the 19th century and few internal features of interest survive. Dee House covers part of the Roman amphitheatre, the northern section of which was excavated in the 1960s. It is bounded on the west by Souters Lane, on the east by St. John's Church and, most recently, on the south by the new County Court building which, controversially, also covers a small part of the buried amphitheatre.

SL

400

1000

1200

1500

1700

*

1800

1900

2000

THE OLD BISHOP'S PALACE
THE GROVES

Occupying a prominent, south-facing, site overlooking the River Dee and The Groves, this large Georgian house was begun before 1745 for Bishop Peploe, but did not become the official residence of the Bishop of Chester until 1865 (the former bishop's palace situated between the Cathedral and the Abbey Gateway was demolished in 1874). Meanwhile, the new house on The Groves was apparently first completed in 1751, then substantially extended later in the 18th century, and further modified in the 19th century. It was the residence of several bishops of Chester. But for many years, from the 1920s, it served as a YMCA hostel until its conversion into commercial offices in the early 1980s.

The exterior, apart from the main door, has been virtually unaltered since the 18th century, and is of red brick with a hipped slate roof. Inside is a six-flight open-well stair with turned balusters (which replaced the original Chinese Chippendale balustrade). This gives access, on the first floor, to a large room (now used as a boardroom) which has fine plasterwork and a mid 18th-century decorated ceiling.

St John's Rectory

3 Vicar's Lane

Also called 'The Old Rectory'. Originally built as the vicarage for the Church of St. John the Baptist, which it faces across Vicar's Lane, it remained as the vicarage until 1957. The building was then occupied by the Grosvenor Club, by which name it is best known locally, although it is presently used as offices. The original Grosvenor Club building, now the HSBC Bank (*qv*), is on Eastgate Street.

Constructed c1750, this three-storey building is in red-brown Flemish bond, with a grey slate roof, and stands on a painted stone plinth. The five windows on the front of the building have rusticated wedge lintels with projecting keystones. A ten-course parapet, with stone cornice, conceals an attic dormer window.

Inside, an entrance hall has replaced the original inner door, but the open-well stair, with curved brackets, survives. Other original details remain on the ground and first floors, but later alterations to the second floor have removed most features.

DN

400

1000

1200

1500

1700

✳

1800

1900

○
2000

ABBEY SQUARE

Most of the buildings on the west and north sides of Abbey Square are individual Georgian houses which were constructed from around 1750 for the Dean and Chapter of Chester Cathedral. They replaced older buildings, such as the brewery and bakery, which had formed part of the monastic complex. Most of the new houses were built between 1754 and 1761, and one has a rainwater head bearing the date 1764. Some on the west side, nearest to the Abbey Gateway, are a little later, although very much in the same style as their neighbours. No 3 is probably dated 1771-2, while Nos 1 and 2 are as recent as 1821-2.

First appearances are, therefore (again) deceptive - these are not conventional 'terraces'! While all the houses are of orange or brown brick in Flemish bond with stone dressings and have low-pitched slate roofs behind brick parapets, they were, in fact, erected over a period of nearly 70 years by several different developers. Even those on the north side, which form the grander of the two terraces, were individually constructed and have minor differences in details such as doors and windows. Nevertheless, despite the lack of uniformity which is displayed in single developments such as Stanley Place and Nicholas Street (*qqv*), Abbey Square can rightly be claimed as

SL

feature of Chester's Georgian houses, including those in Bridge Place and Nicholas Street (*qqv*), that the staircase changed from one side of the house to the other at first floor level.

The central garden is elliptical in plan and was once enclosed by iron railings above the (Grade II-listed) ashlar red sandstone wall. The stone column, which is also listed, is of red sandstone, has a tapering shaft, and is reputed to have come from the Exchange building in Northgate Street when it was demolished in 1862. The cobbles and 'wheelers' (carriage tracks) are a distinctive feature which were the subject of a conservation project in 1981.

the nearest to a formal Georgian square in Chester. Most of the houses are now offices of one sort or another but the internal layout is generally unaltered. Stairs (sometimes richly decorated with three balusters per tread) rise to the first floor within stairwells which continue to the roof, but it's a curious and distinguishing

Apart from the terraces in the Square, there is an isolated building (now the Cathedral Office) on the east side, as well as several other houses, including the Deanery, on the north side of Abbey Street which leaves Abbey Square at its north-eastern corner.

400

1000

1200

1500

1700

**
**

1800

*

1900

O
O
2000

ABBEY STREET

400

1000

1200

1500

1700

Although 'Georgian' in character, this short cul-de-sac leading to the City Walls and the Kaleyard Gate has an interesting variety of properties from several different centuries. Those on the south side (with their backs to the Cathedral) were built between 1826-8 for Mr Thomas of King Street as sub-lessor of the land held by the Rev J T Law.

On the north side, Nos 5 and 7 (dated 1764) together with Nos 9 and 11 (to the rear of No 9) are all large houses built by leaseholders from the Dean and Chapter, and are Listed Grade II*. No 13 is a town house c1720 with later additions and alterations.

Finally, the end house (No 15), closest to the City Wall, is much older. The 18th-century façade is a re-fronting of a 17th-century house which appears to have been built over an earlier stone structure. The rear of the building is largely 19th century and includes a distinctive Gothic arched window with intersecting tracery glazing bars. This building was in a dilapidated condition until 1980 when a major rescue scheme was undertaken which, according to *Conservation in Chester*, used 'every available grant'. The work was beset by structural problems and took 20 months to complete, but the property now provides a series of extremely characterful flats.

1800

1900

2000

CHESTER ROYAL INFIRMARY

CITY WALLS ROAD

Until recently, the original building for the Chester General Infirmary was surrounded by several later extensions, which have now been demolished and replaced by the St Martins development (*qv*).

The hospital was founded as a charitable institution in 1755 following a bequest made for the purpose in 1753 by Dr. William Stratford. At first it was housed in temporary accommodation in the upper part of the Blue Coat School until purpose-built premises could be erected. The new General Infirmary building, which was commenced in 1758 and opened in 1761, faces the City Wall on the west side of Chester, and overlooks the River Dee and the mountains of North Wales. By 1902 it contained 118 beds and had spacious hot, cold, and vapour baths, and all the usual adjuncts of a first class hospital. The word 'Royal' was substituted in 1914 when George V opened the Albert

Wood wing containing six new wards. This and all the other extensions to the old hospital were demolished in 1998 following the progressive transfer of all medical services to the Countess of Chester hospital site on the Liverpool Road.

The main entrance has a projecting porch with two Doric-style columns. Above this is a rounded arch painted with the words ERECTED 1761. The west (main) front is only of two storeys and a basement, but the north, east and south wings, around an inner court, have three storeys plus attics. Construction is in brown brick with grey-green slate roofs. The main internal feature is a large, open-well stone stair, with square balusters. At the time of writing, the building is being converted into luxury apartments by Bryant Homes.

400

1000

1200

1500

1700

*

1800

1900

2000

BRIDGE PLACE
LOWER BRIDGE STREET

Just to the north of the Bridgegate, on the east side of Lower Bridge Street and facing the Bear and Billet, are several fine town houses numbered 1, 3, 5, 7, 9 and 11 Bridge Place. These were built as private residences in the latter half of the 18th century. All are constructed in brown brick in Flemish bond, are of three storeys above basements, and have stone plinths, sills and lintels. They all have slate roofs behind low brick parapets in typical Georgian style.

Number 1 dates from c1770, but No 3 may be of slightly later date. No 5 (Bridgegate House) is a more substantial building which dates from the middle of the 18th century and pre-dates its neighbours. Nos 7 to 11 are late 18th century and have wrought-iron railed forecourts with stone steps leading down to cellar doors beneath the front doors. No 13 was rebuilt c1970 and is a shop which has its south side alongside the City Wall.

All these buildings, except of course No 13, have benefitted from conservation grants as part of the Bridgegate Action Plan of the 1970s. This was the first of the comprehensive conservation programmes to be implemented after the 'Insall Report' of 1968. Nearly £1.5 M was spent in the Bridgegate area over an 8-year period from 1972-79. Ancilliary work included repairing the setts and cobbles in front of Bridge Place in 1972. Bridgegate House was eventually included in the restoration programme in the early 1980s after Chester City Council's threat to serve a Repairs Notice led to the sale of the property.

CHESTER CANAL

For many centuries, perhaps even from before the Roman occupation, Chester had been one of England's main ports, especially for coastal trade to North Wales and also across the Irish Sea to the Isle of Man and Ireland. By the 18th century the increasing size of ships and the relentless silting of the Dee Estuary prompted some major engineering works to improve navigation. Although of limited success, trade by sea remained steady at this time and any decline in fortune was relative only to the meteoric rise of the Port of Liverpool.

It is not surprising therefore that local merchants should wish the Port of Chester to be linked by canals to its hinterland and, in 1772, the Chester Canal Act was enthusiastically supported by the Corporation and many of the leading citizens. The original intention was to link Chester with the new Trent & Mersey Canal at Middlewich, with a spur to Nantwich. It was hoped that this would attract some of the trade from Liverpool and the Midlands, thus countering the threat to the future of the River Dee Navigation and the Port of Chester. Two engineers were appointed: Samuel Weston and John Lawton as his assistant. The then Mayor of Chester, Henry Vigars, performed the ceremony of cutting the first sod at the end of April 1772. The Trent & Mersey company, recognising the implications of the wide-beam barge canal to Chester, then refused permission for the connection at Middlewich. This was a bitter blow for the proprietors of the Chester Canal when they were already suffering construction delays brought about by

engineering and financial problems. The main line of the canal was altered to terminate at a basin and warehouse just outside Nantwich, and the proposed line to Middlewich was now to be a branch.
Five different engineers worked on the 25 km (16 mile) long canal to Nantwich, which was not completed until 1779.

In the decade which followed, the company experienced financial problems due to the lack of traffic, and by 1790 the Chester Canal had fallen into disuse. However, in 1793, work began on another canal – the Ellesmere Canal – which would join Montgomeryshire and the Wrexham iron-producing district to the Mersey Estuary. In 1797 this was linked with the Chester Canal.

At last, 25 years after the first sod was cut, Chester was established as an important canal port. Trade was brisk, a large basin, warehouses, and a canal tavern (qv) were built at Tower Wharf, and the passenger trade from Chester to Liverpool was so popular that it led to the growth of of Ellesmere Port as a fashionable bathing resort.

The success of this totally self-sufficient system depended on good relations between the Chester Canal Company and the Ellesmere Canal Company. An attempted takeover in 1804 failed, but in 1813 the inevitable merger took place and the Ellesmere & Chester Canal Company was formed. The original intention of joining up with the Trent & Mersey Canal at Middlewich was not effected until 1833 - some 61 years after it was first proposed!

CHESTER CANAL
CANAL CUTTING & THE BRIDGE OF SIGHS

The deep cutting carrying the Chester Canal, immediately to the north of the City Walls at the Northgate, is reputed to date from Roman times. The size and depth of the original Roman 'defensive ditch' is uncertain and, although it survived as a town ditch into the 18th century, it is said to have come as a welcome surprise for the contractors who dug the Chester Canal along this line in the 1770s. The resulting ravine through red sandstone

is dramatic from all viewpoints but none more so than from the towpath or a canal boat.

At that time, the ancient Northgate, which housed the City Gaol, still stood (the present Northgate not being rebuilt until 1810). The stone footbridge, known as 'The Bridge of Sighs' connected the old gaol to the chapel of St. John in the south wing of the Blue Coat School, and was used by prisoners taken there from the gaol. According to tradition, condemned felons were led across the bridge to receive their last rites in the chapel - hence, no doubt, its nickname. The slender segmental arch of coarse red sandstone is believed to have been built in 1793 - at about the same time as the Northgate Bridge was rebuilt and the canal was being revived as a going concern. Tall cast-iron railings once flanked the sides of the footbridge to deter any desperate attempts to escape.

CHESTER CANAL

NORTHGATE LOCKS

400

1000

1200

1500

1700

1800

1900

2000

Considerable engineering skills were needed to lift the Chester Canal from sea level on the tidal River Dee up to the level of the Cheshire Plain to enable it to link the city with Nantwich. In addition to the aforementioned cutting, ten locks were built over a distance of 5 km (3 miles) between Chester and Christleton. The first five were situated one after the other on a straight line between a tidal basin at Crane Bank and the Northgate cutting. After obtaining the Chester Canal Act of 1st April 1772, the canal proprietors decided to build a barge canal which required the locks to be 24.4 m (80 ft) long and 4.5 m (14 ft 9 in) wide. It

appears that, due to a clause in the Act inserted by the River Dee Company, the original lock at the bottom of the flight of five was constructed to a width of only 2.1 m (7 ft), no doubt exacerbating the commercial problems in those early years.

When the Ellesmere Canal was constructed in the 1790s, the route north from Chester to Ellesmere Port necessitated a major remodelling of the locks to accommodate a junction between the two canals. The two bottom locks in the flight of five were filled in and the remaining three were rebuilt as the 'staircase' which survives today. Hewn out of solid rock, this impressive feat of engineering lifts boats 10.1 m (33 ft) and is a suitable complement to the deep rock cutting beyond.

Immediately above the locks is a fine example of a lock-keeper's house (now overshadowed by the road flyover), while below, 200 m beyond the sharp bend which is the connection to the former Ellesmere Canal, lie the dry dock, roving bridge and boat-building sheds of Taylor's Yard. Navigation to the river is still possible via the graving dock (alongside the dry dock), the Upper and Lower Dee Basins, and, finally, the Dee Lock beneath New Crane Street.

The various lock structures and the Bridge of Sighs are listed Grade II. The associated warehouses, built from 1792, are described later in this chapter.

SL

400
1000
1200
1500
1700
*
1800
1900
2000

KING STREET
INCLUDING KING'S BUILDINGS

This winding street, once known as Barn Lane, follows a medieval track, dating back to the 13th century or earlier, which led from the Abbey of St. Werburgh to the monks' barn in 'The Crofts'. At the end of King Street, at its junction with St Martin's Way, is a terrace of six Georgian houses, known as King's

Buildings, which were built in 1775–6. For many years this terrace was in danger of collapse, due to settlement, and the walls were shored up with massive timber buttresses, but in recent years the terrace has been restored to its former glory.

Apart from King's Buildings, the south side of King Street especially has many other buildings of 18th century date or even

earlier, although they have inevitably undergone many alterations over the centuries. Nos 1 and 3 date from the end of the 18th century, whilst Nos 5 and 7 are probably of 17th century origin as they were converted into two houses c1720. No 9 is dated 1783 but incorporates a much older building. Nos 11, 11A, and 13 started as a couple of town houses early in the 18th century, but are now offices. Other mid 18th-century town houses are Nos 15 and 17 and Ulver House at No 19. No 21, which is again from the early 18th century, had a new front c1800 and was further restored in 1969–72. Nos 23 and 25 are also small town houses of the early part of the 18th century. On the north side, Nos 6, 14, 18, 32 and 34 are all of 18th-century origin.

FOREST HOUSE

LOVE STREET

Possibly the finest Georgian house in Chester, but now one of the saddest; Forest House was built as a town house for the Barnston family of Crewe Hill. The exact date of its construction is unclear - one reliable source suggests 1759 but others claim 'the 1780s'. Its great height (three tall storeys above a semi-basement) made it a prominent landmark on the skyline of Georgian Chester. It is evident on Hunter's map of the city dated 1789 and on a painting by Moses Griffith c1780. Constructed in the style of Sir Robert Taylor, but not his personal work, the most likely date of construction seems to be the late 1770s or early 1780s.

The surviving building is the central block of a larger house which faced onto Foregate Street. It is three bays wide, built in red-brown brick on a high rusticated stone plinth, and has high pedimented gables. The design is severly classical and was not widely admired at the time; the 19th-century historian Hemingway compared its appearance to that of a public hospital!

Forest House is now but a shadow of its former self. The extensive forecourt and gardens have all been built upon and roads have been made next to the building on two sides. Forest House became auction rooms c1856, a furniture depository c1875, and is now a nightclub.

AVP

400

1000

1200

1500

1700

*

1800

○

○

1900

○

2000

400

1000

SEDAN HOUSE
13 & 13B STANLEY PLACE

1200

The area on the west side of Chester, within the City Walls, comprised large blocks of land occupied by the Franciscan and Dominican friaries (the 'Grey Friars' and 'Black Friars' respectively). For two and a half centuries since the Dissolution much of it lay under-used and undeveloped.

By the 1770s, land was being acquired for a

1500

development of 'genteel modern buildings' as a speculation by the proprietors of the Irish Linen Hall. They began by building in Watergate Street, near to the Watergate, and then progressed rapidly both northward and south-ward.

Stanley Place was built c1780 and is one of Chester's few unaltered Georgian streets. At its corner with City Walls Road are two houses of brown brick using Flemish bond, which began as a single town house. It is the frontage to City Walls Road which is of particular interest and which has given this building its name - Sedan House. The frontage carries a brick porch, standing on a raised stone pavement, and having two doors: one on the north side and one on the south. The west-facing wall between these doors has a nine-pane window. There is a stone step up to the north door and two steps to the south. It was through these doors that the Sedan chair-men entered and left, their passengers having alighted under the cover of the porch to enter the main door. It is believed to be the only surviving example in north-west England.

1700

*

1800

1900

2000

NICHOLAS STREET (WEST SIDE)

400

This fine three-storey terrace with deep basements is the longest and most uniform of any of the Georgian properties in Chester. It is constructed from brown brick in Flemish bond with stone dressings and grey slate roofs to a design by Joseph Turner of Chester (architect of the Bridgegate and Watergate, *qqv*).

This was the final phase of the development undertaken by the proprietors of the Irish Linen Hall

1000

1200

and, like Stanley Place (*qv*), to the north of Watergate Street, it also occupies land formerly owned by the friaries.

Originally built as ten town houses, this terrace subsequently became known as 'Pillbox Promenade', or 'Pillbox Row' because of the number of doctors who had their surgeries there. The last medical practice moved out in 1998 and most of the terrace is now used as offices.

1500

1700

Until the widening of Nicholas Street in 1961-2 to construct the inner ring-road, the street was so narrow that the splendid effect of this terrace could not have been appreciated. Some renovation work has taken place recently, particularly to the ironwork of the stone steps. Although many internal alterations have taken place, as well as the 19th- and 20th-century extensions at the rear, most of the houses still retain fittings dating to the original construction of the terrace.

*

1800

1900

O
2000

THE BRIDGEGATE

LOWER BRIDGE STREET

The earliest crossing of the River Dee was probably a ford which the Romans later replaced by a wooden bridge. This, in turn, gave rise to the present stone bridge which dates from the 14th century. Being the only way into North Wales, the bridge and the adjacent City Walls were originally heavily defended with gatehouses and towers, which are illustrated on old maps.

In the early 1780s, the medieval Bridgegate on the City Walls, which had an octagonal tower and a water tank, was demolished and replaced by the present stone archway designed by Joseph Turner for the Corporation of the City of Chester. Its design is classical and is executed in a yellow sandstone ashlar. There are stone balustrades and, on the south face of the arch are stone bas-reliefs of fasces and a balance. On the north side of the archway, an inscription on marble states that the gate was begun in April 1782 and was finished in December of the same year. The Watergate (*qv*) was also Turner's work.

THE WATERGATE
WATERGATE STREET

As with the other major 'gates', this archway through the City Walls replaced an older, medieval structure. Like the Bridgegate (*qv*), it was designed for the City of Chester by the local architect Joseph Turner after the Corporation had purchased the sergeancy of the old gate from the 12th Earl of Derby in 1778.

The present structure, which is more an ornamental bridge than a gate, was rebuilt at the Corporation's expense in 1788. Like the new Eastgate (1768-9), it is in red sandstone ashlar with a rusticated arch but, unlike the Eastgate or the Bridgegate, it has only one passage for pedestrians. The wall walkway has stone parapets with turned stone ballusters and pedimented central panels. However, unlike the Bridgegate, this archway does not have any inscription or date on it. Its name is derived from it having been the chief access to the ancient Port of Chester when the course of the River Dee was adjacent to the City Walls at this point. It was also the means of access to the wharves at New Crane Street, built after the Dee had been canalised in 1736 and, later, to the basin of the Chester Canal.

400

1000

1200

1500

1700

*
1800

1900

2000

CHESTER CASTLE
GROSVENOR ROAD

Urban analyst David Lloyd has convincingly argued that Chester Castle, as rebuilt from 1788 by Thomas Harrison, comprises the finest group of county buildings in England. The composition is of three main blocks, the centre one containing the marvellous Assize Court (now Chester Crown Court), fronted by a double hexastyle portico and with, originally, the county prison behind.

The impetus for this major work came from the Justices who shared the widespread concern about the dilapidated condition of the medieval castle. Both the Great Hall, which had been converted into a Shire Hall, and the gaol were particularly unworthy and inadequate. The Justices decided on new buildings and in 1785 a public competition was announced.

The competition was won by Thomas Harrison, then of Lancaster. Construction commenced in 1788, but the final complex, which also included barracks, armoury, and an entrance gateway or *propylaeum* (*qv*), was not completed until 1822. Harrison may have devised the final arrangement of buildings early in the proceedings, but initially the medieval Shire Hall and other structures were to be retained to avoid using temporary accommodation during the improvements. The ultimate scheme occupied an area much greater than the original castle compound, with the Barracks and *propylaeum* built well beyond the medieval castle wall. Yet Harrison took care to maintain a relationship between the new buildings and the remaining medieval structures, with the Agricola Tower and the tower of St Mary's Church balanced about the principal façade.

SL

400
1000
1200
1500
1700
1800
1900
2000

The gaol, which was demolished in the 1930s to make room for County Hall (*qv*), was set back-to-back with the courts along the change in ground level. Work on the Sessions House started in 1791, the portico being erected in 1797, and the interior being completed in 1801. The two wings flanking the parade ground, barracks, and armoury, were planned in 1801 and built in 1804.

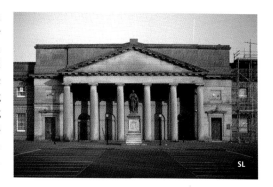

A number of themes that preoccupied Harrison throughout his life are manifest in the design of the Castle. The overall layout is Palladian in derivation, but the composition is neo-classical and the details Grecian. The portico was the first major application of a primitive Greek Doric order in England, its twelve massive monoliths later much admired by C R Cockerell who shared with Harrison an obsession with the expressive qualities of stone.

The Shire Hall itself is the centrepiece. Its semi-circular form, 24.4 m (80 ft) in diameter, 13.4 m (44 ft) high, with 12 Ionic columns supporting a semi-dome roof, was described by Hemingway as having 'an imposing effect upon the spectator and gives a proper dignity to the seat of justice'. Recently restored by local architect Simon Johnson of the Biggins Sargent Partnership, this magnificent interior, now known as 'Court No 1', is well worth visiting on the occasions when the Crown Courts are opened to the public.

The Cheshire Military Museum now occupies part of the north wing, while the former Officers' Mess in the south wing, and Napier House (facing the Agricola Tower), stand empty awaiting new uses.

400

1000

1200

1500

1700

*
1800
●

1900

●
2000

TELFORD'S WAREHOUSE

RAYMOND STREET

The large brick buildings which stand between Raymond Street and Tower Wharf date from the late 18th and early 19th centuries - after the canal system was extended to the River Mersey at Ellesmere Port.

The warehouse, which is partly on land and partly over the water, is ascribed to Thomas Telford, the canal company's engineer. It was constructed over the canal to allow boats to be loaded or unloaded from the full height of the loading bay within the building. Construction is of brown brick in English garden wall bond beneath a hipped grey slate roof with boldly projecting boxed eaves in Telford's manner. The building was sensitively converted into a public house and restaurant in the mid-1980s by local architect James Brotherhood. It was severly damaged by fire in 2000 but is currently being restored.

The adjacent building, which is L-shaped in plan, was built as the Ellesmere Canal Company's Offices and Canal Tavern; then used as the Tarvin Rural District Council Offices, more recently as 'Diocesan House', and now (having 'gone full-circle'), is British Waterways' Border Counties headquarters. The front part of the building, facing Raymond Street, is the original canal company office dating from the 1790s, while the rear wing was added c1815. This was the tavern built for the benefit of passengers using the Liverpool-Chester Packet Boats, often as part of a long and arduous journey from England to Ireland or America.

TH

400

1000

1200

1500

1700

*
1800

1900

2000

LEADWORKS' SHOT TOWER

LEADWORKS LANE

400

1000

1200

1500

1700

1800
✱

1900

Although lead had been mined in Wales and worked by the Romans during their occupation of Chester, the Leadworks dates from the end of the 18th century. The Shot Tower was built in 1800 by Walkers Maltby & Company for the manufacture of lead shot for use in the Napoleonic Wars. Since the demolition of a similar shot tower on the south bank of the Thames in London, following the Festival of Britain (1951), the Chester tower is the only one still standing in Britain.

The manufacture of lead shot in tall towers by the use of gravity had been patented in 1782 by William Watts, a Bristol plumber who developed the process in the tower of St Mary Redcliffe Church, Bristol. The molten metal drops become spherical as they fall through the air, solidify as they cool, and are caught in a barrel of water at the base of the tower.

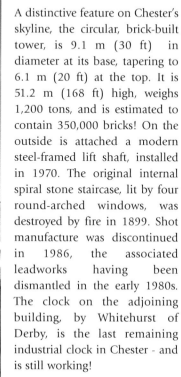

A distinctive feature on Chester's skyline, the circular, brick-built tower, is 9.1 m (30 ft) in diameter at its base, tapering to 6.1 m (20 ft) at the top. It is 51.2 m (168 ft) high, weighs 1,200 tons, and is estimated to contain 350,000 bricks! On the outside is attached a modern steel-framed lift shaft, installed in 1970. The original internal spiral stone staircase, lit by four round-arched windows, was destroyed by fire in 1899. Shot manufacture was discontinued in 1986, the associated leadworks having been dismantled in the early 1980s. The clock on the adjoining building, by Whitehurst of Derby, is the last remaining industrial clock in Chester - and is still working!

AVP

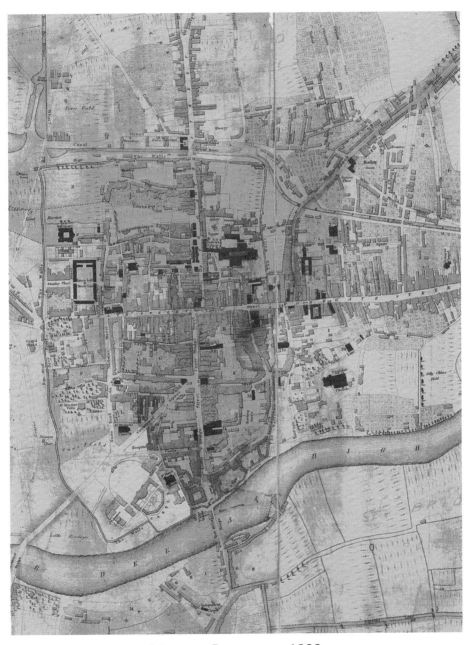

MAP OF CHESTER IN 1833
(EXTRACT FROM MAP BY JOHN WOOD)

CHAPTER 9

VICTORIAN EXUBERANCE
1801 - 1900
GRAHAM FISHER

Visually, the 19th century is the most astonishing in Chester's history. It began with one creative genius, Thomas Harrison (1744-1829), whose work ultimately provoked a reaction that paved the way for another, John Douglas (1830-1911). Yorkshire-born Harrison had won the competition to rebuild and civilise Chester Castle in 1785, a task that was to occupy him until 1822. Stylistically, the resultant neo-classical complex (gaol, courts, barracks, etc) with its quite exceptional regard for function, is perhaps only rivalled by Liverpool's St George's Hall. Among the scattering of classical stone buildings from the early years of the 19th century, Harrison's really stand out - the Chester City Club, originally the Commercial Newsroom of 1808, and the Northgate, its dark austerity appropriate for the site's desolate past as the city gaol. But it is his final project, involving the first major break (Grosvenor Street) in the

Roman gridiron street pattern, which is yet another masterpiece: the Grosvenor Bridge, with its awesome single-span arch across the Dee, took six years to build and was not opened until 1831 - two years after Harrison's death.

There is a gentle irony in that it was a Harrison pupil, the Wrexham-based Thomas Penson, who not only evolved his own version of Jacobean architecture but also produced a son, T M Penson, who was to launch the half-timber revival in Chester. Before 1830, Eastgate Street had been a largely Georgian street of modest scale. It is Penson's rather unremarkable work at Nos 36-38 which began (as almost a first in Britain) a black-and-white obsession which has had us in its grip ever since. The newly formed Archaeological Society enthusiastically approved, calling for the return of the 'rich and lively façades, the curiously carved fantastical gables,

Riverside at Boughton

which distinguished the brief but gay rule of the Stuarts' while condemning the 'miserable brick, and incongruous piles of heavy Athenian architecture which has characterised Chester's more recent past'! And in 1862 the founder member James Harrison [no relation] was asked to reconstruct the threatened 17th-century half-timbered God's Providence House in Watergate Street. James Harrison, like Penson, could turn to a variety of

styles: his impact on St Michael, St Mary-on-the Hill, and Holy Trinity (now the Guild Hall) is impressive, while his Savings Bank of 1853 entertainingly essays Tudor gothic, impertinently looking over to his namesake's Castle. Penson's similarly playful Militia Barracks were nearby but have been demolished and replaced by the 1967 Constabulary Headquarters.

A more serious loss in the 1960s was the wonderfully exuberant mid-Victorian Market Hall's façade. This had once made a fine partner for W H Lynn's Gothic Town Hall (1869), with Gilbert Scott's thoroughgoing Cathedral restorations of the 1870s completing a quintessential 19th-century city centre. Visitors arriving at Francis Thompson's splendidly composed Italianate General Station (1848) would have witnessed great changes in the middle years of the 19th century, but even they might not have been prepared for the subsequent transformation of the central streets, the most dramatic in any English historic city.

The black-and-white revival initiated by Penson was to reach new heights in the hands of his pupil T M Lockwood and, above all, in the sophisticated response from John Douglas, born in Sandiway the year after Thomas Harrison had died. Lockwood was responsible for the vigorous Victorianisation of The Cross, light-heartedly turning the Eastgate/Bridge Street corner (1888), applying Renaissance ornament opposite a few years later, and turning the century with the former Owen Owen's on the north side of Eastgate Street. In Foregate Street the inventive Old Bank Buildings are Lockwood at his best, aesthetically competing under the Grosvenor patronage with the most concentrated of Douglas displays - the iron turret for the Eastgate clock, the Flemish-gothic of the Grosvenor Club (1883), and the brilliant east side of St Werburgh Street (1895-7), commended by Edward Hubbard for 'the loving care lavished on the timber detailing making it as fine as anything of its kind within the entire vernacular revival movement'. Just as captivating is the architect's earlier symphony in brick for Grosvenor Park Road, leading to Edward Kemp's outstanding Grosvenor Park. The prolific Douglas (giving character also to the Eaton Estate villages) had established that the century's architectural sensitivities could take many forms...

BUILDING   PAGE

Commercial Newsroom *(1808)* 142

Castle Gateway *(1811-22)* 143

Watergate House *(1820)* 144

Grosvenor Bridge *(1827-33)* 145

Miln's Seeds - Steam Mill *(1834)* 146

Browns of Chester *(1828 and 1858)* 147

Chester College Chapel *(1844-47)* 148

Derby Place, Hoole *(1840s - '50s)* 149

Chester General Station *(1847-48)* 150

Deva Terrace *(1850s)* 152

Sandown Terrace *(c1850)* 153

Lower Park Road, Queen's Park *(1850s)* 154

Trustee Savings Bank *(1851-53)* 155

33 Eastgate Street - Natwest Bank *(1859-60)* 156

Queen Hotel *(1862)* 157

God's Providence House *(1862)* 158

Town Hall *(1865-69)* 159

Albion Street & 'The Albion' Public House *(1865-69)* 160

St Werburgh's Mount *(1873-74)* 162

St Paul's Church *(1876)* 164

Grosvenor Park Road *(1879-80)* 166

HSBC Bank - formerly Midland Bank *(1881-83)* 167

The Queen's School *(1882-83)* 168

The Grosvenor Museum *(1885-86)* 169

The Cross buildings *(1888-92)* 170

Parker's Buildings *(1889)* 172

Christ Church, Newtown *(1893-1900)* 173

2 - 18 St Werburgh Street *(1895-97)* 174

Walmoor Hill *(1896)* 175

'Coniston', Newton Lane *(1898)* 176

Eastgate Clock *(1897-99)* 177

City Baths *(1898-1901)* 178

Shoemakers' Row *(1897-1909)* 179

COMMERCIAL NEWSROOM (CHESTER CITY CLUB)
NORTHGATE STREET

MP

Thomas Harrison was responsible for a brilliant series of civic buildings in the Greek revival style in the centres of Liverpool, Manchester and Chester. Opening, in June of 1808, first as the Commercial Coffee Room and later the Commercial Newsroom, his building next to St Peter's Church is stylistically characteristic with its attractive ashlar facing. Above three rusticated arches, four Ionic columns carry a pediment. Simple decorative panels are included above the three tall windows which light the double-height room within. The principal room (originally the newsroom but now a fitted billiard room) has a barrel roof and an apsidal end. The ground floor was, in fact, built as shops with glazed arches, but in the 1960s the shopfront was moved back to create an extension of the walkway through Shoemakers' Row - the starkly contrasting 'black and white show' to the north. Passageways on both sides of the Newsroom lead to St Peter's Churchyard, a peaceful oasis which in its linking of secular and spiritual represents townscape perfection. The Commercial Inn (now the Commercial Hotel), also by Harrison, reminds us of the name of its more auspicious neighbour.

The early subscription City Library moved from White Friars to the Newsroom in 1815. Its entrance fee rose to five guineas, ensuring a select clientele, but ultimately its bookstock was transferred to the Mechanics' Institute, precursor of the 1877 Free Public Library which stood in St John Street until 1984. Meanwhile, the Newsroom was managed by a committee representing the 'proprietors', with the mayor, local MPs and leading military officers automatically entitled to use the facilities. During the second half of the 19th century the Newsroom evolved into the Chester City Club, which it remains to this day.

Photo Survey

MP

400

1000

1200

1500

1700

1800

*

1900

2000

CASTLE GATEWAY

GROSVENOR ROAD

The grand entrance, or *propylaeum*, was the last phase of Thomas Harrison's rebuilding of the Castle complex, not fully complete until 1822. David Lloyd says 'especially when seen in some lights with the main Castle buildings in the background, it seems the nearest thing to great poetry in architecture ever achieved in Chester, at least since the time of St John's or possibly of the Cathedral choir stalls'- a view not altogether shared by the polemical Victorians later in the century!

As with much of Harrison's work, there is the feeling of suppressed energy, his tough neo-classic designs never slipping into conformist academicism. This massive gateway in the Greek Doric order, flanked by two smaller pedimented lodges, is in every respect a real entrance, a sublime approach to justice or ceremony, to civics or car-parking. Reminiscent of the Brandenburg Gate in Berlin (1789-93), Harrison's Chester version is said to have been inspired by the propylaea at Athens and the Temple of Theseus. There is evidence that Harrison's contemporaries were impressed even if some thirty-five years later the newly-formed Archaeological Society was (incredibly!) attacking these 'incongruous piles of heavy Athenian architecture'.

400

1000

1200

1500

1700

1800

*

1900

2000

400

1000

1200

1500

1700

1800

*

1900

2000

WATERGATE HOUSE
WATERGATE STREET

Originally a single and substantial town house, Watergate House was built in 1820 for Henry Potts to the designs of his friend Thomas Harrison. Potts was Clerk of the Peace for the County of Cheshire and as such was closely involved in the building of the County Court at Chester Castle, part of Harrison's masterpiece which took over thirty years to build.

The construction is of Flemish bond in brown brick with stone dressings. The roof is of grey slate. From the outside, Watergate House can be seen to have a basement over which are two storeys. Although the main part of the building is of square plan, it has

an unusual octagonal entrance hall, to which one gains access through an Ionic doorcase by ascending a flight of six curved stone steps. The entrance hall, which is lit from a domed sky-light, gives access to the principal rooms through curved doors. A stone staircase, with moulded iron balusters, leads to the upper floor.

Now in use as offices, it was for many years the headquarters of the Cheshire Community Council, and before that had been the headquarters of Western Command since 1907.

GROSVENOR BRIDGE

400

1000

1200

1500

1700

1800

＊

1900

'The superb Grosvenor Bridge has real personality; it speaks for itself and has form, dignity and repose. Of all the buildings in Chester it is the one which gives most unqualified pleasure'. Such was the verdict of Alec Clifton-Taylor who went on to admire the bridge's wonderful span, a single segmental arch of 61m (200 ft) rising high above the Dee, and the (mostly) creamy-grey sandstone from the Peckforton Hills which has weathered so well. And Ian Nairn, arguing that this was Thomas Harrison's masterpiece, pointed out that nothing could better illustrate the difference between building classical design as a fashion and understanding its essence than 'the superbly handled niches and the brilliant idea of accentuating the tension by having the arch voussoirs in a lighter stone'.

The decision to build an additional bridge across the Dee was taken in 1818 as one element in the improvement of the road to Holyhead. Harrison submitted several plans, including schemes for iron and three-arched stone bridges, before the single span stone arch (the largest in Europe at the time) was selected. Construction began in 1827 and was left in the very capable hands of William Cole Jun. and engineer Jesse Hartley after Harrison's death in 1829. No less than Telford, Rennie and Brunel all had some involvement as consultants during the project.

The new access road, Grosvenor Street, drove diagonally through the Roman street plan, which had hitherto survived within the City Walls. It was symbolically fitting that the bridge's somewhat premature formal opening in 1831 should have been by Princess Victoria, as these developments were trailers for Chester's astonishing Victorian years.

The architect's stone model for the Grosvenor Bridge, restored and re-sited by Chester Civic Trust in 1979, may be seen on the grassy bank below the City Wall, beside Castle Drive.

MILN'S SEEDS ('STEAM MILL')
STEAM MILL STREET

AVP

The coming of the canal in the 1770s, its extension to the Mersey at Ellesmere Port in the 1790s, and its eventual linkage to the national network in the 1830s, were key factors in the early industrial growth of Chester. Viewed from City Road, the 'Steam Mill' (well renovated by James Brotherhood and Associates) and the uniquely surviving 1800 Leadworks' Shot Tower (*qv*) on the opposite bank of the canal are effective punctuation points in this evocative industrial townscape.

The building now known as the 'Steam Mill' was formerly a seed warehouse dating from 1834, rebuilt after a fire (c1864) and substantially extended at the turn of the century.

The Steam Flour Mill was, in fact, on the opposite side of Steam Mill Street where operations began in the 1780s - shortly after the Chester Canal was opened in 1779. The surviving buildings on this site, which are also listed Grade II, were constructed in three phases in the early and mid 19th century. U-shaped in plan, the middle section includes cast iron columns which are believed to have been part of the original steam-powered mill.

AVP

Frances Aylmer Frost (a successful flour miller whose family became very prominent in Chester's local government) bought property on Canal Side in the 1820s and is believed to have commissioned the new warehouse. The tower bore the name 'F A Frost & Sons' until the business was taken over by 'Miln's Seeds' at the end of the 19th century. Internally, the building was notable for a blown-air seed transport system, all of which was removed after closure in 1986. The void left by the machinery is now an impressive atrium serving six floors of offices. The ground floor includes a restaurant and bar.

400

1000

1200

1500

1700

1800

*

●

1900

●

2000

BROWNS OF CHESTER
28-34 EASTGATE STREET

In the early years of the 19th century Chester was a relatively prosperous county town, with a thriving retail base. Eastgate Street was being compared with London's Regent Street and its star attraction was Browns' store, nicknamed the 'Harrods of the North'. Browns of Chester, now part of the Debenham Group, originated in a millinery and haberdashery shop kept by Susannah Brown in the late 18th century.

in the Eastgate style wars which within thirty years were to place contrasting buildings by T M Penson on each side of them!

That on the right, known as the 'Crypt Building' (1858), is arguably Penson's most successful work in Chester. The choice of sandstone and Early English Gothic is a deliberate attempt to harmonise with the medieval undercroft over which it was built (see p. 71).

This contrasting pair of buildings , both built for Browns, epitomises the battle of the styles which raged in Chester in the middle of the 19th century. On the left, the severely classical building (1828), on the site of the Honey Steps (where honey used to be sold), is where the firm made its big impact, much admired by Chester historian Joseph Hemingway. The two Greek revival Doric columns on the Eastgate Row are described by Pevsner as 'unexpectedly solemn' - perhaps they are anticipating extinction

By 1860 the classical revival was well and truly out of fashion, but Chester is fortunate in having Browns 1828 building, and Lewis Wyatt's Lloyds Bank on the corner of St John Street as modest accompaniments to the great works of Thomas Harrison.

400

1000

1200

1500

1700

1800

1900

2000

CHESTER COLLEGE CHAPEL
PARKGATE ROAD

Chester College was founded in 1839 on land donated for the purpose by the Dean and Chapter of Chester Cathedral. At that time the population of Chester was only about 23,000, but the Diocese and its educational responsibilities encompassed both Manchester and Liverpool. Remarkably, this was the first purpose-built teacher training college in England and would soon be described by one of Her Majesty's Inspectors as 'a model for every other'.

The main building, on the corner of Cheyney Road and Parkgate Road, was completed in 1842 and the College Chapel was added between 1844 and 1847.

The architect is J E Gregan of Manchester, but Pevsner and Hubbard (The Buildings of England: Cheshire) add that the chapel was partly built, and the fittings almost entirely made, by students of the college, who were, in Ruskinian manner, instructed in manual labour and crafts, a forge being provided on the premises. It is perhaps not surprising that the

College's first Principal, The Revd. Arthur Rigg, was considered a leader in technical education at the time.

The building is rock-faced in coursed red sandstone, with a spired bell turret at the south west corner. There is an ashlar interior, with a steep hammerbeam roof, a tiered west gallery, and rows of stalls facing each other.

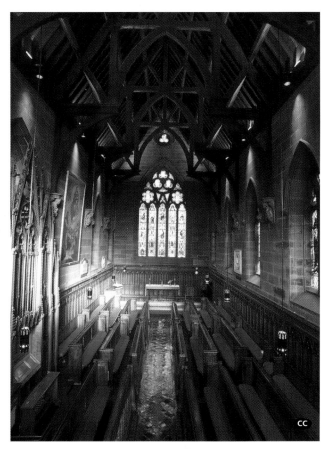

CC

400
1000
1200
1500
1700
1800
*
1900
2000

DERBY PLACE, HOOLE

OFF HOOLE ROAD

Railways arrived in Chester in 1840, bringing more people and greater prosperity, as well as a significant increase in the physical size of the city.

Suburbs grew up close to the station to meet the needs of railway workers and those in associated trades. Street after street of terraced houses was built in the open fields. The town houses of Derby Place, which are in pairs or groups of three, are among the finest of this period in the new suburb of Hoole. Built from brown brick in Flemish bond under grey slate roofs, many still have their original features and are listed for their group value.

Brian Harris commented in his ground-breaking City Guide that 'for the student of suburban domestic architecture, Hoole presents curious contrasts in styles'. It repays exploration with its still quite appealing shopping centre in the Faulkner Street-Charles Street-Westminster Road area while, on the edge, the attractive Derby Place perhaps represents the end of an unreflecting classical tradition in its forceful unpretention.

AVP

1847-8 • Listed Grade II*

CHESTER GENERAL STATION

STATION ROAD

Like Derby and Shrewsbury, Chester Station was a true 'joint venture', although collaboration between the competing railway companies often did not extend far behind the scenes (*cf* more recent times!). The four commissioning companies were the London & North Western Railway, the Shrewsbury & Chester Railway, the Chester & Holyhead Railway, and the Birkenhead, Lancashire & Cheshire Junction Railway. Sites closer to the city centre were considered before deciding on the apparently open fields on the edge of Chester, bordering the parish of Hoole - where, in fact, there was a market garden and a small group of cottages, from which a shoemaker had to be forcibly evicted!

Francis Thompson chose a strong Italianate style (shades of the contemporaneous Osborne House), with a long frontage block of 354 m (1,160 ft) in dark-coloured fire-bricks, relieved with Storeton stone facings and dressings and sculptured decoration by John Thomas. Following the destruction of the Trijunct station at Derby, Chester General Station must stand as Thompson's masterwork, the original iron trainshed being designed by C H Wild with Robert Stephenson involved in his capacity as Chester & Holyhead engineer. The building contractor was the amazing Thomas Brassey, who was born locally, near Aldford; Chester was an important step in his career as one of the world's leading railway building contractors.

MP

400

1000

1200

1500

1700

1800

1900

2000

Visual impact is provided by the boldly treated, slightly projecting blocks at each end of the entrance façade, both arched on the ground storey and crowned with a pair of round-arched turrets. Railway station historian Carroll Meeks saw Vanbrugh's influence in this usage of towers, considering the mid-century decades a period when 'horizontality and verticality seem to be in equilibrium'. On a more practical note, the large clock was originally centrally placed but later moved to the left so that it could be seen by would-be passengers coming along the new City Road (1864) without the Queen Hotel (1862) then blocking the view.

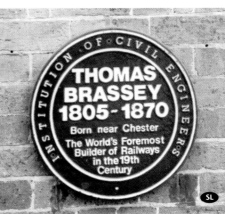

1

400

1000

1200

1500

1700

1800

*

1900

2000

DEVA TERRACE

This terrace of 17 three-storey houses, across Dee Lane from the south east corner of Grosvenor Park, stands squarely on the river bank and looks across the Dee to the Meadows. It is the only range of houses to lend a touch of formality to the two miles of richly varied riverside landscape between the Roodee and the countryside upstream of Chester.

The terrace was built on a narrow tongue of land, perhaps a former sandstone quarry, between the river and the cliff-like bank to the north. The houses stand behind a lawn with white cast iron railings to the water. The façade is a late example of Georgian style: the warm red brickwork is in Flemish bond, enlivened by white-painted door-cases and sashes, and the roof is of the grey Welsh slate common to most of Chester's 18th- and 19th-century buildings.

LM

SANDOWN TERRACE

OFF BOUGHTON

This handsome Italianate terrace, originally three substantial houses, has a tower at each end. Its frontage, facing Boughton, is of two storeys but the sloping site enables the basement rooms to open onto the garden at the rear, giving the full three storeys a commanding view of the river and the Meadows beyond.

The brown brick construction in Flemish bond is greatly enlivened by large areas of painted stucco. The ground floor at the front has three projecting Roman Doric porches above which the 12-pane sash windows are embellished with stucco architraves and ornate entablatures. The south elevation, facing the garden, has a first floor balcony and cast iron verandah.

As with Queen's Park on the opposite bank of the Dee, Sandown Terrace indicates growing suburban prosperity in the wake of the arrival of the railways in Chester.

400

1000

1200

1500

1700

1800

*

1900

2000

153

400

1000

1200

1500

1700

1800

*

1900

2000

1-17 LOWER PARK ROAD

QUEEN'S PARK

Increasing prosperity, albeit slow until the arrival of the railways, coupled with the cramped and sometimes insanitary conditions in central Chester, encouraged the middle classes to look further afield for their new houses. The farmland on the south bank of the Dee had obvious attractions - particularly as it was upwind of the industrial activity around the canal and railway yards!

Queen's Park was a villa estate laid out in the mid 19th century by Enoch Gerrard, who bought all the land when it was advertised for sale in 1851.

James Harrison, the dominant day-to-day operator in Chester between Thomas Harrison and John Douglas, designed some of the houses. A suspension bridge was built over the river in 1852 and in 1856 Thomas Hughes in his *Stranger's*

Handbook to Chester warmly praised the new development: 'The salubrity of the air, and the high commanding situation of Queen's Park, together with its beautiful river scenery, and its close proximity to the city, combine to render it peculiarly suitable for villa residences'. The sweeping roads were indeed to be lined with large villas in their own spacious grounds.

In fact this initial optimism was quite short-lived. Between 1851 and 1861 some 48 houses were built but only 12 more were added over the next 30 years. The roads have since been filled and those few Italianate villas (with riverside gardens originally designed by Kemp) do handsomely survive in Lower Park Road.

1

400

1000

1200

1500

1700

1800

*

1900

2000

TRUSTEE SAVINGS BANK
(NOW THE PAPARAZZI RISTORANTE)
GROSVENOR STREET

James Harrison won a competition in 1847 for a design for a Savings Bank in Tudor style: the building opened six years later, cheekily looking across to Thomas Harrison's Greek revival edifice at the Castle. In their *Buildings of Chester*, Morriss and Hoverd (1993) saw this Tudor Gothic as a forerunner of the timber-framed revival. The Classic certainties had indeed gone even if James Harrison altogether lacked the gothic scholarship for which Pugin was crusading. The former Bank's detailing is good, with clever massing of the main elements making for a memorable Grosvenor Street corner. The cheerful clock turret at that corner has a clock by Joyce of Whitchurch. The building was extended to the south in the 1970s and is now a restaurant.

33 EASTGATE STREET (NATWEST BANK)

400

1000

1200

1500

1700

1800

*

1900

2000

This is a first-rate classical stone building, with a pediment and giant order of Corinthian columns. But how, as late as 1860, did its promoters have the courage (or impertinence) to build it in Eastgate Street when the black-and-white revival was clearly underway? Thirty years later, local writer G A Audsley had no doubts that George Williams's

building represented 'a style of architecture distinctly out of place in such a street', and indeed Williams's subsequent work in Chester was to be (wildly over-the-top) half-timbered.

Peter de Figueiredo has explained that when Messrs Dixon and Wardell, proprietors of the Chester Bank, decided in 1857 to build their prestigious headquarters in Eastgate Street, they were keen to introduce a metropolitan character to the city. The fact that they were bankers to Thomas Brassey, who was by then becoming one of the world's greatest railway contractors, may have helped to give them the confidence to ignore the disparaging remarks of the Archaeological Society. Further, they determined to stop off Eastgate's north Row, with its somewhat seedy reputation, rather than run it through their new building. Despite opposition to the proposed closure, they obtained approval from the City's Improvement Committee by offering a strip of adjoining land for widening St Werburgh Street (*qv* Nos 2-18 St Werburgh Street).

QUEEN HOTEL
STATION ROAD

Neatly dressed in their scarlet uniforms, the porters from this rather grand Victorian hotel met passengers from all the trains and escorted them to their rooms across the road. The hotel, designed by T M Penson, had its own telegraph office and was linked to the Queen Commercial Hotel (now The Town Crier) on the opposite corner by an underground passage. Architecturally though, Pevsner was none too impressed: 'this is four-storeyed and Italianate, with a big porch, the whole composition stodgy as these Italianate hotels tend to be'.

The hotel was first built in 1860-1, a dozen years after the opening of the General Station to which it was linked by a covered way (the enclosed space remains but is no longer available to passengers). An extensive fire led to a rebuild the following year, again by T M Penson, an architect who could confidently work in black-and-white. or gothic, romanesque, or renaissance, as the occasion demanded. For this 1862 version, which dispensed with its original high roofs, he was joined by Liverpool's Cornelius Sherlock. The added Art Deco porch on City Road is unfortunate.

400

1000

1200

1500

1700

1800

*

1900

KT

●
2000

GOD'S PROVIDENCE HOUSE
9 WATERGATE STREET

This building, more than any other, symbolises changing architectural attitudes in Victorian Chester and deserves a footnote in any study of the roots of 'conservation consciousness'. It virtually replaces a 1652 original whose unsound structural state was to coincide with the vociferous debates about the city taking place in the newly-established Archaeological Society. In 1857 its Journal had attacked the 'miserable brick, and incongruous piles of heavy Athenian architecture' of the preceding century, calling for a return to the spirit of the 'rich and lively façades, the curiously carved fantastical gables, which distinguished the brief but gay rule of the Stuarts' that had characterised the earlier city. Concern was expressed for the future of God's Providence House but, at a December 1861 meeting, it was pointed out that the new owner, Mr Gregg, 'with a commendable regard for the venerable spot, and in deference to the public wish, had determined to preserve the front part, and keep up as much as possible its ancient character'. Mr James Harrison (the first architectural correspondent of the Society) 'had effected the happy design before them, by which he had adapted the premises to modern improvement and uses, but had left the ancient work in all its purity'. In fact the house was completely rebuilt and the height greatly increased, quite altering its impact on its Georgian neighbours. The re-use of some of the old carved timbers does not make this other than a Victorian building, further emphasised by the mechanical plaster detailing which enriches the façade.

TOWN HALL
NORTHGATE STREET

WH Lynn's Town Hall at Barrow-in-Furness has been described as a distinguished follower of Manchester Town Hall, but his earlier work at Chester makes this building an exciting precursor to Waterhouse's masterwork. The Belfast architect won a competition here with a £100 prize for a building that was to be 'substantial and economical rather than of an ornamental character', avoiding styles 'incompatible with the general features of this Ancient City'. The cost was not to exceed £16,000, a stipulation that had to be overlooked… Chester urgently needed something imposing after the 1862 fire which had destroyed the 1698 Exchange.

High Victorian gothic in form, the Town Hall's central tower rising 49 m (160 ft) is ornately elaborated with a diagonally-set spire. An elevated entrance is impressively approached from a double flight of steps. Ian Nairn found the façade forbidding, but engagingly described the planning of the central hall and staircase as 'delightful spatial toy - the stern Victorian father playing passionately at model railways in his bedroom'.

Apart from the over-spend (both in the architect's estimate and the contractor's tender), building work was interrupted by a strike among the stonemasons who had fallen out rather badly with the Clerk of Works! The project took four years to complete instead of the planned two, but was nevertheless opened with great ceremony by the Prince of Wales accompanied by the Prime Minister, W E Gladstone. On 27th March 1897 the Council Chamber was destroyed by fire, but was restored in the following year by the Chester architect T M Lockwood.

Electric lighting was installed in 1896. Lockwood designed a suspended ceiling for the Assembly Room which was installed between 1899-1902; this improved the lighting and the acoustics whilst hiding the original roof.

400

1000

1200

1500

1700

1800

*

1900

O
2000

400

1000

1200

1500

1700

1800

1900

2000

ALBION STREET AND INN

Twenty years ago (in the 1980s) Chester City Council promoted a conservation scheme in this small housing area near the city centre. During the first half of the 19th century the area was a pleasure garden behind the former Albion Hotel in Lower Bridge Street (see Park House). The hotel and its garden were sold in 1865 and the land was developed, providing a Welsh Chapel, a Drill Hall for local volunteers, and 52 houses, mainly terraced, of which 42 survive. It was accepted that the houses were not architectural masterpieces, but that they did have a unity of design (red brick with simple geometrical patterns in cream-coloured brick) and a strong Victorian character.

On the corner with Park Street, overlooked by the City Wall, is the Albion Inn whose traditional stance complements the community spirit of the development.

A classic street-corner pub, the Albion is arguably the last remaining unspoilt Victorian pub in Chester.

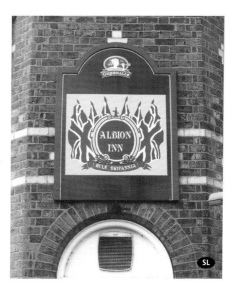

The present Licensee has had his name 'over the door' for the past 30 years and the Albion has retained the traditional three-room layout covering Vault, Snug and Lounge Bar. A superb Victorian cast-iron tiled fireplace holds a roaring coal fire in winter and is complemented by the William Morris wallpaper all around. Britannia and cast-iron sewing machine tables abound and etched glass sash windows remain. Great War artefacts and pictures give a distinct period feeling, along with posters and bright enamelled advertising signs.

Albion Street and the adjoining Volunteer Street both lead to the former Drill Hall (listed Grade II), which was a recruiting centre during the First World War. Many a young lad would have spent his 'King's shilling' in the bar of the Albion before going to face the horrors of the Western Front. A dwindling band of 1914-18 Veterans are still to be seen having an occasional noggin when special commemorative events are held.

400

1000

1200

1500

1700

1800

✱

1900

●

2000

400

ST WERBURGH'S MOUNT
ST WERBURGH STREET

1000

1200

St Werburgh's Mount was the name given to a house which stood opposite the south transept of the Cathedral. Its last occupant was Thomas Hughes, author of *The Stranger's Handbook to Chester*, the City's best Victorian guide. The present building of 1873-4 is a group of shops behind a street-level arcade designed by local architect, John Douglas.

1500

This was one of Douglas's very first projects in the city centre, some 20 years before his masterly east side of St Werburgh Street, but still with charm and individuality. The effect is 'cottagey', with herringbone brickwork between the timbers, chunky chimneys, and pargetting in the gables. Similar plasterwork

1700

1800

*

1900

2000

patterning is evident in T M Lockwood's No 20 Bridge Street, both architects almost certainly being influenced by W E Nesfield's Crewe Green cottages of the mid-1860s.

It was the 'old-fashioned sweet shop' rather than the significance of the building or its site that led to this nomination by local schoolchildren.

400

1000

1200

1500

1700

1800

*

1900

2000

ST PAUL'S CHURCH
BOUGHTON

With its almost Rhine-like setting above the bend of the Dee, this is a church of great vitality from architect/parishioner John Douglas. The unexpectedly broad, short shape is evidence of William Cole's 1830 classical predecessor, parts of which were incorporated in the rebuilding. The high arcading of the nave, with posts and pointed arches entirely of timber, has been described symbolically as a forest glade. Beyond, through the wrought-iron screen and above the altar, we look up to the attractively painted decoration and the stunning William Morris (Edward Burne-Jones) window. There is a sensitive Arts and Crafts feel to the whole interior, which was extended by Douglas in 1902.

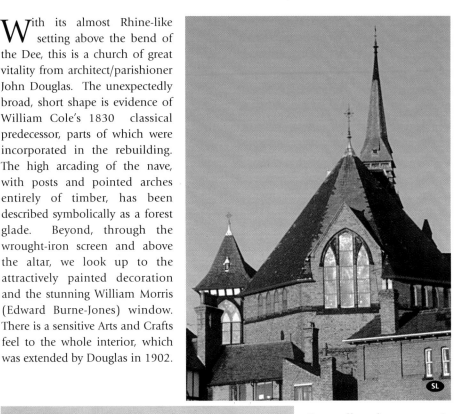

Externally the story is different. The locally produced Ruabon red pressed brick, which is used uncompromisingly here, may not be to everyone's taste but the silhouette of the high red roof, which sweeps down in one pitch over both nave and aisles, is an impressive sight when viewed from the Meadows.

400

1000

1200

1500

1700

1800

*

1900

2000

400

1000

1200

1500

1700

1800

✱

1900

2000

GROSVENOR PARK ROAD

'How much more convincing Douglas is where the temptation to fussiness inherent in the magpie technique is avoided' - thus wrote Sir Nikolaus Pevsner when appraising this astonishing symphony in brick. It is a brilliant group, the composition varied yet enough of a unity. The octagonal turrets at either end of the range, the enormous hipped gable, the steep roofs, the ribbed chimney stacks: the overall character is Germanic. The terrace was built with Douglas himself as developer and landlord. Railings and shrubberies edged the road as an extension of Grosvenor Park, Douglas having designed the lodge at the main entrance. This approach scheme was compromised on the west side, but the east, complete with Baptist Church (now Zion Chapel) from Douglas at the same time, is unrivalled street architecture.

HSBC BANK

(FORMERLY THE MIDLAND BANK) 47-57 EASTGATE STREET

Originally housing the Grosvenor Club and (at street level) the North & South Wales Bank, this richly detailed and decorated building is surely another masterpiece by the ubiquitous architect John Douglas.

Standing just inside the City Wall immediately adjacent to the Eastgate, this 1880s building is a tall four-storey gable in red sandstone and red stone-dressed brick beneath a Westmorland green slate roof. The design shows a distinctly Flemish influence, although this was to be more strongly executed in Douglas's design for the Cheshire Constabulary Headquarters at 142 Foregate Street in 1884.

The Grosvenor Club and bank were extended in 1908 by Douglas and Minshull and, although more Germanic in character, the complete building has a marvellous quality and harmony.

Note the Grosvenor portcullis carved in the lintel above the door, the shields bearing the arms of the 12 former shires of Wales, the gilt metal coat of arms of the Grosvenor family high up on the building and, last but not least, the date '1883' at the very top.

400

1000

1200

1500

1700

1800

*
1900

●

○
2000

THE QUEEN'S SCHOOL
CITY WALLS ROAD

Deceptively 'Douglasian', though perhaps lacking his degree of conviction, the Queen's School was, in fact, designed by E A Ould, a pupil and assistant in Douglas's office during the 1870s. The commission may have been influenced by John Douglas and his patron, the Duke of Westminster, to give encouragement to the young man at the outset of his independent career.

The original building, on the site of the old city goal, is L-shaped, the south wing facing City Walls Road and the north wing facing Bedward Row. Construction is in brown brick with red terracotta and stone dressings. The west elevation is richly detailed in the vernacular revival style including mullioned windows, shaped chimneys, and an ornate steepled belfrey. Note also the terracotta figure of Queen Victoria set in a niche above the former main entrance.

Ould went on to design the exuberant Uffington House overlooking the river from Dee Hills Park (1886) before joining the Liverpool architect G E Grayson to form the partnership of Grayson & Ould in 1887 (when still only aged 34!).

GROSVENOR MUSEUM
GROSVENOR STREET

400

1000

1200

1500

1700

T M Lockwood's building is of red brick, with stone dressings. It is in a free Renaissance style, with Dutch gables. Four local organisations had come together in the 1880s to establish a joint committee to see how a museum could be operated. They were the Chester Archaeological Society, the Chester Society of Natural Science, Literature and Art, the School of Science, and the School of Art. A public meeting was held at the Town Hall to launch a subscription fund: the Duke of Westminster subscribed £4,000 and donated land he owned for a portion of the proposed site.

The foundation stone was laid by the Duke in February 1885 and the building was opened in August 1886. A large extension was built in 1894 and a neighbouring house (No 20 Castle Street) was incorporated in the museum in the 1950s. The millennium was celebrated by major refurbishments which now permit access to the lecture theatre and the lower floors by people with disabilities.

Collections of carved Roman stones, Chester silver, and local paintings are among the Museum's finest assets, but the permanent displays and temporary exhibitions also provide a fascinating introduction to the development of the city over 2000 years.

1800

1900

2000

THE CROSS BUILDINGS

There are those who find it ironical that The Cross, focus of the Roman gridiron of streets, should now be such a sumptuous 19th-century show. The perpetrator is T M Lockwood (for the first Duke of Westminster) whose black-and-white revivalism is invariably bigger and brasher than any of the 16th- and 17th-century originals. The Eastgate Street/ Bridge Street corner of 1888 has all the conviction needed for its somewhat whimsical fantasy. While its forms are more knowledgeable than, say, Penson's earlier 19th-century Eastgate Street half-

timber, Lockwood's work tends to lack the sophistication of John Douglas. His project here thoroughly swept away the past, replacing a timber-framed building which incorporated the 16th-century cistern. This corner was featured on a 1975 Architectural Heritage Year postage stamp; it must be photographed as much as Douglas's Eastgate Clock (*qv*), itself the most photographed clock in the UK after that in Westminster.

Four years later, in 1892, the Duke gave Lockwood the chance of rebuilding the opposite (Watergate Street) corner of Bridge Street. Here there is a combination of half-timber with brick, but also typical Renaissance ornament and round-headed centre window lights, influenced by Norman Shaw's (1873) New Zealand Chambers in London's Leadenhall Street. Donald Insall's mould-breaking 1968 conservation report bafflingly suggested that this corner was unworthy of its important position in the pedestrian network of the Rows....

400

1000

1200

1500

1700

1800

*1900

O
2000

PARKER'S BUILDINGS
FOREGATE STREET

Until late in the 19th century this area was among Chester's most crowded, with residential courtyards and passages leading off on both sides of Foregate Street. In this context, Parker's Buildings were socially enlightened, the tenement form being copied from work then being done by housing trusts in London to provide acceptable accommodation at reasonable rents. It was built to house retired workers from the Eaton Estate where C T Parker served as land agent to the first and second Dukes of Westminster from 1881 until 1911. He had a formidable reputation as a meticulous manager, seemingly most demanding of the estate's most prolific architect, John Douglas. Parker complained here of poor construction - 'smoky chimnies are an intolerable nuisance' - and delay in rectifying his complaints.

KT

But it was Parker himself who had consulted the Improved Industrial Dwellings Company, arranging for Douglas to view their London work. Edward Hubbard has commented that 'although too late in date to have pioneering historical significance, it nevertheless provides a rare departure from Douglas's usual building types: the result was a three-storey block containing 30 flatted dwellings, with stairways enclosed within the building but open to the air'. Two separate blocks, each with one shop, flank the approach.

400

1000

1200

1500

1700

1800

1900

2000

CHRIST CHURCH, NEWTOWN
GLOUCESTER STREET

The terraced streets of Newtown were developed very much in the wake of the railways. The original Christ Church, by Thomas Jones, served that community from 1838; John Douglas's first plans for a rebuild date from 1876. However, the design was amended considerably (a tower and spire never materialised) and most of the work took place in the 1890s. This much under-rated church shows the Late Victorian subtleties of which Douglas was capable. These effects are complemented by the unexpectedly cheerful chancel fittings and rood beam introduced by Sir Charles Nicholson in the early 20th century. Nicholson, a member of the Art Workers' Guild, was consultant architect to seven cathedrals and had been one of five finalists in the Liverpool Anglican Cathedral Competition of 1903.

SL

400

1000

1200

1500

1700

1800

*
1900

●

2000

2-18 St Werburgh Street

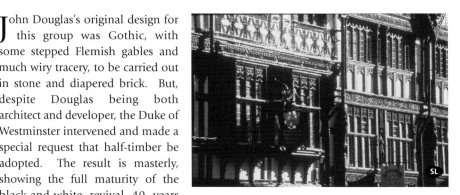

John Douglas's original design for this group was Gothic, with some stepped Flemish gables and much wiry tracery, to be carried out in stone and diapered brick. But, despite Douglas being both architect and developer, the Duke of Westminster intervened and made a special request that half-timber be adopted. The result is masterly, showing the full maturity of the black-and-white revival 40 years after its local 'origins' just over the road with Penson's work in Eastgate Street.

Edward Hubbard, in his The Work of John Douglas, perfectly celebrated the achievement: 'In this work, the city's half-timber revival reached its very apogee. Above the shop fronts is an unbroken expanse of gorgeously ornamented half-timber. Although the long elevation is diversified by no less than eleven gables, it is broken down into five separate units, each a complete composition in itself and with its own individuality. It is the loving care lavished on the timber detailing which makes St Werburgh Street as fine as anything of its kind within the entire vernacular revival movement'.

Douglas himself had bought the whole length of the street to prevent its being haphazardly developed after the Corporation had demolished the old row of shops so as to widen the approach to the Cathedral from Eastgate Street. Alas, as in so many buildings in the city centre, the upper stories are no longer fully utilised.

1000

1200

1500

1700

1800

＊
1900

2000

WALMOOR HILL
DEE BANKS

John Douglas's own house, built after working some thirty productive years from a Chester/Eaton Estate base, is testimony to a regional career of very high achievement. The house, late gothic to Elizabethan in style, is placed on a sandstone outcrop with a commanding view over the Dee; its castellated walls take full advantage of the steeply sloping site. The main entrance is in the form of a porch with an oriel window above (a small private chapel within) and an octagonal turret to the side. Over the porch is featured a lion supporting the Douglas family banner flanked by a pair of headstops of Edward VII and Queen Alexandra. A statue of Queen Victoria (commemorating her Diamond Jubilee of 1897) is set in a canopied niche on the river side. Inside, the finely carved woodwork imparts great character to the hall and staircase. So many features testify to Douglas's national and domestic pride, despite his own personal tragedies (his wife and four of his five children predeceased him).

On Douglas's death in 1911, Walmoor Hill was left to his only surviving son. Subsequently it became a College for young ladies, a preparatory school for boys, and the Headquarters of Cheshire Fire Brigade. Latterly it has been in private ownership. Nearby, on the opposite side of Dee Banks, is a Gothic pair of houses by Douglas from 1869, one of which he built for himself not too long after his arrival in the city.

1000

1200

1500

1700

1800

*
1900

○
○

○
2000

Photo Survey

400

'CONISTON'
NEWTON LANE

1000

1200

Designed and built by H A Clegg, as a family home for his own use. Clegg was a master stonemason, who made many of the monuments in Overleigh cemetery (including his own). His craft is evident in the door and window surrounds. Although Clegg died soon after the house was completed it remained in the possession of his family until 1920. This is one of the few domestic houses in the Arts and Crafts style in the district. The ornate leaded glass frontage conceals an interior arched entrance and was perhaps an afterthought. Interior passageways are floored with Minton tiles. The land on which the house was built was part of the Kilmory Estate, then surrounded by nursery gardens.

1500

1700

1800

1900

2000

EASTGATE CLOCK
EASTGATE STREET

Chester's medieval Eastgate, with its pointed archway and battlemented tower, was taken down in 1766. The rebuild of 1768-9, attractively preserving the circuit of the City Walls, was by a Mr Hayden at the expense of Richard, Lord Grosvenor.

Given the strong Victorian character of Eastgate Street (prior to 1850, Georgian brick had predominated), it is most appropriate that John Douglas's cheerful design for the clock turret was accepted in

commemoration of the Queen's Diamond Jubilee in 1897. Not that this was his first attempt at designing the Eastgate Clock. The idea was very much alive in 1881 when Douglas designed the Grosvenor Club (*qv*) adjacent to the Eastgate and again in 1884 when a masonry clock tower was suggested. The proposed tributes to Queen Victoria were many, varied, and fiercely contested, but Edward Evans-Lloyd ('citizen and Freeman') eventually prevailed and so the Eastgate finally got its clock.

The open wrought-iron structure (quite different from the various unexecuted designs) was made by Douglas's cousin, James Swindley of Handbridge, and the clock itself by J B Joyce of Whitchurch. Although the clock is dated 1897 it was actually unveiled in a civic ceremony in 1899.

400

1000

1200

1500

1700

1800

1900

2000

CITY BATHS

UNION STREET

400

1000

1200

1500

1700

1800

1900

2000

Public baths were established in 1849 in Tower Road outside the north west corner of the City Walls. By 1883 they had been replaced by a floating bath on the Dee which, during a flood in 1899, broke from its moorings and became stranded above the weir. It was replaced in position, but did not last long after the opening of the new City Baths in 1901. This is a building which (like the 1848 General Station and 1863 Market Hall)

suggests some conflict between functional interior and 'architectural' façade. Hubbard has argued that the aesthetic implications of the unfamiliar building type were not logically pursued. The structure (with its 'Atlantic' and 'Pacific' pools) is based on a competition-winning design by Harold Burgess of Kensington. However, it was local architect John Douglas who finished the job, fronting the building with a characteristic domestic elevation, engagingly working in brick, stone and half-timber. It is as much of its time as the 1970s'

Northgate Arena (which thankfully hasn't totally replaced it), although we can perhaps see why its split-mindedness might irritate the more ideological 20th-century modernist.

SHOEMAKERS' ROW
NORTHGATE STREET

Shoemakers' Row, between Thomas Harrison's Commercial Newsroom and the Market Square, was rebuilt at the turn of the century as part of a City Corporation road widening project. There has been considerable criticism of the development since it involved replacing a true (if ramshackle) Row with a covered walkway just above street level. John Douglas designed several of the new black-and-white buildings (Nos 5-13, probably No 19, and Nos 27-31), but, not being responsible for the whole design, could not achieve that masterly combination of picturesque diversity with visual order which characterises his contemporary scheme for the east side of St Werburgh Street (*qv*). James Strong, a pupil of Douglas, designed Nos 15-17 (replacing the Cross Keys Inn), in which the somewhat whimsical semicircular oriel windows were repeated a couple of years later in his design for the 1911 Fire Station closer to the Northgate. No 25 was the Woolpack Inn; this was probably partially rebuilt by Douglas in 1903 but refaced c1914 to a 1909 design by Strong. Cheshire County Architect Henry Beswick (a pupil of Lockwood) was responsible for No 3 and Nos 21-23, the earliest parts of this group.

400

1000

1200

1500

1700

1800

*
1900
*

2000

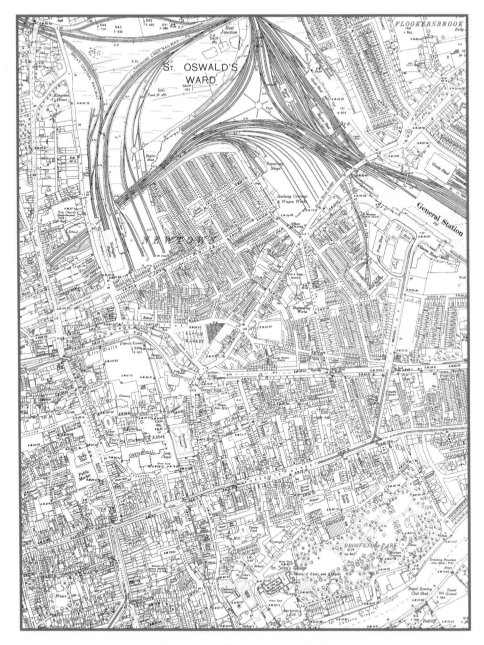

MAP OF CHESTER IN 1911

Reproduced from the Ordnance Survey 25 inches to 1 mile map, courtesy of Chester City Council

CHAPTER 10

EXPANSION, DEMOLITION, CONSERVATION
1901 - 2000

PETER DE FIGUEIREDO AND CYRIL MORRIS

The 20th century has been marked by enormous changes in commerce, retailing, traffic, leisure, and tourism, largely within the personal knowledge of our readers. All these factors have had a huge impact on the built environment of the city.

For the first few years of the new century the exuberant architecture of late Victorian Chester continued, unaffected by the national taste for architectural grandeur. When, for example in 1911, the Duke of Westminster erected St Michael's Row in Bridge Street in the Baroque style, and faced it in white and gold tiles, there was such a public outcry, that he took it down and rebuilt a half-timbered façade. John Douglas continued to work in the vernacular revival, demonstrating at 1-11 Bath Street (1903) his skill at picturesque composition.

From 1910 the pace of building gradually diminished, whilst the two world wars and the intervening depression of the 1930s significantly limited new building in the first half of the century. Notable during this period, however, was Maxwell Ayrton's St Werburgh Row (1935) and the Odeon Cinema (1936), as well as further distinguished half-timbered buildings such as the Manchester and Liverpool District Bank in Foregate Street (1921) (now the Royal Bank of Scotland) and the George and Dragon Public House (1931).

By 1945 the City Engineer and Surveyor, Charles Greenwood, was preparing a 'Plan for Redevelopment', which concluded that two problems needed urgent attention - slum clearance and traffic. The solution was to be demolition and redevelopment, together with an inner by-pass. However, in his preface to the report, the mayor, Alderman Matthews Jones commented that 'Happily ours is not the problem of the blitzed cities. Our task is to preserve rather than rebuild'. But the scale of neglect had left whole areas such as Lower Bridge Street and Watergate Street in decay. Extensive slum clearance took place behind the Town Hall and in Newtown, whilst the inner ring road swept away Egerton House in Upper Northgate Street and the Unitarian Meeting House known as Matthew Henry's Chapel. By 1963 The Chester Chronicle concluded that 'the agents for change are the

The Bell Tower

motor car, the Corporation (with its new market hall and north-west central development and inner ring road), the private developers (office blocks and shops) and Grosvenor Laing (with their £3M plan for a covered shopping precinct)'. The Chronicle's opinion was that the latter was a modern variation on an original and unique Chester notion (the Rows). But in the construction of the precinct, surviving walls of the Roman bathhouse were swept away, much of it unrecorded.

Recognising the pressures for redevelopment, the City Council appointed George Grenfell Baines and the practice he founded, Building Design Partnership, to prepare a planning study of the Central Area (published 1964) and to provide a planning consultancy which influenced development from 1960 to 1975.

It was a time of change and destruction, and for Chester the defining moment came in 1968 with the publication of a Conservation Study commissioned jointly by the government and the City Council. Donald Insall was the farsighted author, and his recommendations for the care and protection of the city were enthusiastically taken up. In 1969 the City Conservation Area was designated, and a specific sum (the product of a 2d rate) was allocated for the establishment of a Conservation Fund. In 1971 the country's first Conservation Officer was appointed. During the next 20 years the emphasis was on saving historic buildings, and finding new uses to ensure their continued viability. But for the Conservation Programme, buildings such as Gamul House, Kings Buildings, The Falcon Inn, and the Dutch Houses would have been lost. Over 600 buildings were

restored, and the success of the programme was recognised by two prestigious Europa Nostra Awards, in 1983 and 1989.

Many sensitive new buildings were fitted in where gaps had appeared in the street scene. But whilst Chester's success in conserving old buildings is unmatched, modern architecture has failed to find popular favour. All too often the result has been the safe option of a replica façade or a building relying on the use of design details poorly adapted from the past. Happily there are exceptions. The Constabulary Headquarters (1967) is a suitably bold and uncompromising neighbour to Thomas Harrison's great neo-classical Castle complex. C & A's store (1970) and the Chester Magistrates' Court (1991) show how modern architecture can respond sensitively to a historic setting. The Scout Headquarters (1999), cast up on dry land at the Old Port, makes witty reference to Chester's maritime history.

In the last decade of the century, attention turned to resolving the impact of traffic and to improving environmental conditions. The introduction of a Park and Ride system and pedestrianisation of the city centre have made Chester a more pleasant place to visit. Life in the centre has also improved, and demand has increased for new houses and the adaptation of upper floors of old buildings for living 'over the shop' Two decades after publication of the Insall report, the report 'Conservation in Chester' concluded in 1988, 'Conservation is not about living in the past; it is the creation of an environment within which our architectural heritage can survive for future generations'.

BUILDING   PAGE

1 - 11 (and 13) Bath Street *(1903)* — 184
Ye Gardeners Arms *(1907)* — 185
Sealand Road United Reformed Church *(1909)* — 186
Love Street School *(1909)* — 187
St Michael's Row & Arcade *(1910-11)* — 188
Hydro-electric Station *(1913)* — 190
Westminster Coach and Motor Car Works *(1914)* — 191
Royal Bank of Scotland *(1921)* — 192
Queen's Park Suspension Bridge *(1923)* — 193
George & Dragon Public House *(1931)* — 194
St Werburgh Row *(1935)* — 195
Odeon Cinema *(1936)* — 196
The Newgate *(1938)* — 198
County Hall *(1938-57)* — 199
The Grosvenor Precinct *(1965)* — 200
St Martin's Gate *(1966)* — 202
Constabulary Headquarters *(1967)* — 203
C & A Store *(1970)* — 204
Pepper Street Car Park *(1972)* — 205
Cathedral Bell Tower *(1975)* — 206
Northgate Arena *(1977)* — 207
Shipgate Development *(1985)* — 208
Marks & Spencer Financial Services *(1988)* — 209
Grosvenor Court *(1989)* — 210
Rufus Court *(1991)* — 211
Chester Magistrates' Court *(1991)* — 212
The Forum / T J Hughes *(1970 and 1993-96)* — 213
Scout Headquarters *(1999)* — 214
St Martins *(2000)* — 215

1903 • Listed Grade II

1 - 11 BATH STREET
AND NO 13, 'THE SPINNEY'

A row of six cottages designed by John Douglas who developed the site himself. It is built of stone with circular turrets and steep gabled roofs in a fairy book Gothic style, and is one of the architect's most original compositions - a delightful surprise found in a modest back street. On the corner with Foregate Street is the former Prudential Assurance Building by Douglas, erected at the same time. Douglas was determined to create good street architecture in Chester, and this is one of several speculative developments he built to show how it could be achieved.

No 13 Bath Street is a small town house, again by Douglas in 1903, which continues the fairy-tale style in hard red Ruabon brick. This was to have formed part of a projected street linking across to Grosvenor Park Road but the plans seem to have been abandoned in 1906.

YE GARDENERS ARMS

33 CHRISTLETON ROAD

Designed by J H Davies & Sons for the Albion Brewery, then situated in Seller Street, Chester. Nationwide, breweries were striving to improve the image of their public houses so as to attract customers from a broader band of society. Their aim was to make every new pub a truly well crafted building, warm, welcoming, comfortably furnished, and able to reflect something of the imagined ease and security of an earlier age. Ye Gardeners Arms is one of the least altered of such inns in Chester.

The ground floor is of banded red and buff sandstone, the oak doorway has long consoles and a Tudor-arched head. The first floor and the gable above are timber-framed with shaped plaster panels; the casements are leaded. The interior is panelled in oak and has beamed ceilings. Internal doors have been removed, but each of the three licensed rooms (with fires in winter) retains an individual character. This is still a real 'local'.

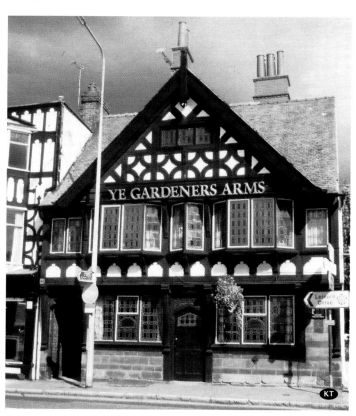

400

1000

1200

1500

1700

1800

1900

*

2000

400

1000

1200

1500

1700

1800

1900

*

2000

SEALAND ROAD UNITED REFORMED CHURCH
WHIPCORD LANE

Also called the 'Tin Tabernacle'; this modest single-storey structure was built to accommodate a small congregation which used to worship in the Sealand Road area, hence the official name. This type of construction, of corrugated iron with wooden windows, was commonly used at that time for inexpensive buildings such as mission churches. It is a rare surviving example. Another survival is a former Mission on Walker Street, Hoole, now used as a furniture warehouse.

LOVE STREET SCHOOL
LOVE STREET

The best of several new schools erected for the City Council in the early years of the century, and designed by Henry Beswick. Built in hard red brick and yellow terracotta, its institutional character is moderated by a skilful and well-grouped composition. The three-storey block facing Forest Street has a striking furnace-chimney expressed as a campanile, with a timber-framed bell-cote attached. The entrances were from Forest Street, boys on the left, girls on the right. It is now used as offices.

St Michael's Row and Arcade

31-35 Bridge Street

This huge black-and-white building was erected for the 2nd Duke of Westminster and replaced a Victorian building only 40 years old. It was designed by William Lockwood, son of the architect Thomas, and was the subject of a keenly fought civic campaign.

As first erected in 1910, it was wholly faced in white and gold Doulton tiles in a vaguely Baroque style, but this led to strong public opposition. So, in March 1911, following petitions from the City Council and the Bishop, backed up by letters in the press, the Duke agreed to demolish and re-erect the front in the favoured vernacular revival style, and in consequence a quantity of white Doulton tiles was put up for sale in the local newspaper. The cost of reconstruction, estimated at about £4000, was charged to the Duke's personal

account. Below Row level the tile-clad frontage was retained, as was the elegant tiled arcade reached by the modern steps from Bridge Street.

Built by local contractors, John Mayers & Co, the structure has a steel frame, and in the process of rebuilding, Lockwood managed to add an extra floor.

The entrance was remodified in 2000 with new steps leading from Bridge Street.

400

1000

1200

1500

1700

1800

1900

2000

HYDRO-ELECTRIC STATION
CASTLE DRIVE

Mills have existed on the site since before 1275. In 1910 the City Corporation, having purchased the site, decided to remove the old Dee Mills.

An electricity supply for Chester had been inaugurated in 1896 but in 1911 the maximum load had been reached on the steam-powered station, which adjoined New Crane Street. In the same year the City Electrical Engineer, S E Britton, submitted a scheme to the Lighting Committee for the erection of a hydro-electric plant on the site of the old Dee Mills.

His plans were criticised by the Chester & North Wales Architectural Society, which approached the Corporation suggesting that the designs were out of harmony with the Old Dee Bridge. The Society offered their advice, proposing that the building be designed in a style more appropriate to the gothic arch of the bridge. The present sandstone building is the product of that collaboration.

When built it was the only hydroelectric plant in England which dealt with both tidal and headwaters, a design which was later adopted for York in 1923. When hydro-electric generation ceased at Chester, the building was used after 1951 as a pumping station to extract water from the river.

MP

WESTMINSTER COACH AND MOTOR CAR WORKS
NORTHGATE STREET

400

1000

The origins of this building are a little unclear and may be somewhat earlier than the attributed date of 1914. The façade of elaborately moulded terracotta and red brick was designed by Philip H Lockwood and is believed to have been built in 1913-4 for the Westminster Coach and Motor Car Works. However, the site was already occupied by J A Lawton & Co, Coach & Carriage Builders, whose premises were badly damaged, but not completely destroyed, by a fire on 1st July 1910. Contemporary photographs of the fire and its aftermath show a very similar front elevation, albeit one storey higher, to that which exists today. Whether fully or partially rebuilt, it seems unlikely to have been as much as four years after the fire.

The motor car works subsequently became a car showroom and continued as such until the early 1970s. From 1973-9 the building was occupied by the Chester Arts and Recreation Trust. A new library was built in 1981-4, replacing the former library in St John Street which had opened as a Free Library in 1874. The dominant, arched elements of the restored façade are reflected in the modelling of the interior of the new building. The Library was designed by the Cheshire County Council's Department of Architecture and received a Civic Award in 1987. It is now destined to become Chester's new Market Hall.

1200

1500

TH

1700

1800

1900

TH

2000

400

ROYAL BANK OF SCOTLAND
15 FOREGATE STREET

1000

The former premises of the Manchester and Liverpool District Bank, this is one of the most accomplished examples of the half-timber revival in Chester, where the style long continued in fashion. The architect was Francis Jones of Manchester. Built of a sturdy oak frame with jettied gables, decorative panels, oriels and tall mullioned windows, it is a vituoso display within a well-orderded composition. It is well worth looking inside, for the intimate banking hall has oak panelled walls, a beamed ceiling, and a little gallery. The four-storey section facing Frodsham Street, labelled Bank Chambers, is an extension of 1964 by Saxon Smith and Partners.

1200

1500

1700

1800

1900

*

●

2000

THE QUEEN'S PARK SUSPENSION BRIDGE
THE GROVES

The present pedestrian bridge, completed in 1923, replaced an earlier one built in 1852 by Enoch Gerrard. The previous bridge was built to provide a short route between the centre of Chester and the new residential suburb of Queen's Park (see Lower Park Road)

By 1920 Gerrard's bridge, which had been built and maintained privately, had become unsafe and it was decided that a new and wider one was necessary. The present graceful structure, with a span of 84 m, was built by David Rowell & Co Ltd in a style more typical of the second half of the 19th century and contrasts with the solid stone arches of the Old Dee Bridge and Grosvenor Bridge.

1

400

1000

1200

1500

1700

1800

1900

2000

400

1000

1200

1500

1700

1800

1900

*

2000

GEORGE & DRAGON
UPPER NORTHGATE STREET

A late flowering of the half-timber revival, the pub was erected for the Birkenhead Brewery Company on a triangular site at the junction of two arterial roads. Unlike most vernacular revival roadhouses of the 1920s and '30s, this is not just a cursory reference to the 'olden days', but a really strong design, assembling a plethora of decorative motifs, jetties, leaded lights, and oak boarded doors into a coherent and original composition. The interior has been largely spoiled in typical brewery manner, but on the traffic island in front stands a splendid original timber signpost of the saint spearing a writhing dragon. At the time of writing this too is, sadly, under threat as part of a modernisation scheme - but plans to replace the signage are being resisted by the Chester Civic Trust.

ST WERBURGH ROW
ST WERBURGH STREET

A row of shops and offices built for the Hodkinson Trustees under the shadow of the Cathedral in 1935. The architect was Maxwell Ayrton, designer of the Wembley Stadium with its famous twin towers, and an expert on reinforced concrete design. In St Werburgh Street the Roman Doric piers of the colonnade are of concrete, but the building is otherwise in a sensitive Arts and Crafts style, with a sweeping Westmorland green slate roof and white rendered walls. An exemplary piece of street architecture, it shows how a simple modern building can sit happily in the most historic setting.

400

1000

1200

1500

1700

1800

1900

*

2000

400

1000

1200

1500

1700

1800

1900

*

●

2000

ODEON CINEMA
NORTHGATE STREET

Photo Survey

An Art Deco cinema tailored to the sensibilities of a historic city, the Odeon Chester foregoes the usual streamlined cream and black tiles in favour of hand-made brick. The style however, remains recognisably 'Odeon' and it is one of the best works of Harry Weedon, the company's architect, and his assistant Robert Bullivant. It has a prominent site in the Town Hall Square, and at the top of the corner tower the characteristic red neon sign glows bright, the only neon lettering permitted in the city centre. The foyer survives little altered,

SL

with Art Deco staircases and light fittings, and original tubular metal furniture. Although the auditorium has been sub-divided, a visit to the lower cinema still gives an idea of the former 'picture palace' interior.

400

1000

1200

1500

1700

1800

1900

2000

THE NEWGATE
PEPPER STREET

400

1000

1200

1500

1700

1800

1900

2000

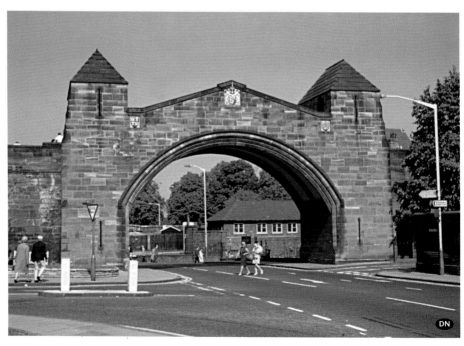

One of two 20th century gates though the City Walls, the Newgate was built in 1937-8, to the design of Sir Walter and Michael Tapper. It stands alongside the 17th-century Wolfgate and was built to permit traffic around the south side of the city centre. Two massive stone towers of vaguely Gothic character flank Pepper Street, and are connected by a steeply curved archway. From the top, there is a good view of the half-excavated Roman amphitheatre.

COUNTY HALL

CASTLE DRIVE

Built on the site of Harrison's gaol at Chester Castle (*qv*), County Hall was designed in the late 1930s in a neo-Georgian style favoured for many public buildings of that era. Work stopped in 1940 after completion of the concrete frame structure of the ground and part of the first floors.

In 1947 the basement and ground floor were brought into use but it was not until 1954 that approval was received to complete the building to the design of the County Architect, E Mainwaring Parkes. The original proposal for a pitched roof was replaced by a parapet and flat roof; the building was, unusually, completed with a steel framed structure on the existing two floors of reinforced concrete.

The external facing materials - Wattscliffe stone and Stamfordstone grey facing bricks - were selected in 1938 by Sir Giles Gilbert Scott (architect of Liverpool Cathedral) for a fee of one hundred guineas. The stone coat-of-arms above the entrance was carved by the Liverpool sculptor, H Tyson Smith.

SL

400

1000

1200

1500

1700

1800

1900

2000

1

400

GROSVENOR-LAING PRECINCT
EASTGATE STREET / BRIDGE STREET / PEPPER STREET

1000

The first proposals were announced in 1961 when the executors of the Eaton Estate proposed a shopping mall or precinct linking up with their earlier St Michael's Arcade. The precinct, together with the inner ring road and the development behind the Town Hall, were the three big redevelopments of the '60s in Chester. Detailed plans were published in 1963 by the Grosvenor-Laing Partnership and their architects Percy Thomas and Son.

1200

The subsequent demolition and excavation resulted in the loss of important Roman remains and a row of Georgian houses in Pepper Street. However, the revitalisation of the

1500

backlands of Eastgate Street South and Bridge Street East incorporated the existing Rows into the precinct in an imaginative way and without disturbing the historic façades. With links from Eastgate Street, Bridge Street, Pepper Street, and the City Walls, the scheme included shops, offices and a multi-storey car park. Apart from Pepper Street, where the original scale was totally altered by the precast concrete and glass façade, and the view of the car park from the City Wall, most of the development is tucked away unobtrusively behind the buildings that were there before. The local name for the development was soon abbreviated to The Grosvenor Precinct.

1700

SL

1800

1900

*
○
○
2000

Twenty years later there was an extensive remodelling and, within the last year, following a change in ownership and name (now The Grosvenor Shopping Centre), a further major refurbishment. This latest has included new steps at the Bridge Street entrance to St Michael's Arcade, a new canopy over the Eastgate Street entrance, and a major alteration to the Pepper Street façade. On Pepper Street the original stained glass panels were removed, but happily The Chester Civic Trust recovered them and has stored them for possible re-use. Although the provision of a lift at Pepper Street has improved access for shoppers, the architectural treatment of both this and the Eastgate Street entrance is not an improvement.

400

1000

1200

1500

1700

1800

1900

2000

400

1000

1200

1500

1700

1800

1900

*

2000

St Martin's Gate
St Martin's Way

The controversial construction of the dual carriageway inner ring road resulted in the loss of several listed buildings (of which Egerton House on Upper Northgate Street was the most notable) and the piercing of the City Walls.

The footbridge, designed by A H F Jiggins, City Engineer & Surveyor, in conjunction with the city's Consultant Architect George Grenfell Baines of Building Design Partnership, is a most successful solution to a peculiarly difficult problem.

The circuit of the City Walls is carried over the roadway by a high-level lightly cambered concrete footbridge which is obviously modern in both outline and construction, yet is successfully integrated with the ancient wall on either side.

1967

CONSTABULARY HEADQUARTERS
NICHOLAS STREET

400

1000

1200

1500

1700

1800

1900

2000

This building has been the subject of controversy since proposals for the site became known. The Royal Fine Art Commission and The Chester Civic Trust criticised the scheme. On the other hand the Insall Report of 1968 cited the building as an example of beneficial change within the city. Mr Insall found the scheme to be well related to Grosvenor Street and the Castle.

textured concrete gable wall by William Mitchell, framing the view of the Combermere Monument of 1865 by Marochetti provides, in the opinion of the Civic Trust when it gave the building an Award in 1969, "a particularly successful link with the Castle opposite".

Designed by the County Architect, Edgar Taberner, it makes an important and positive townscape contribution and is sited in a competently handled landscape setting designed by Derek Lovejoy & Partners. Whilst it makes no stylistic concessions to its neighbours, the

Despite this notable award, the building continues to arouse controversy. Changes to the array of antennae at roof level and a lack of maintenance of the pool features flanking the main entrance, have detracted from its appearance in recent years. At the start of the 21st century, the future of the building is uncertain. The Police Authority plans to move its headquarters to a central site in the county and increasing land values in the city centre pose threats to the survival of the building.

400

1000

1200

1500

1700

1800

1900

✱
2000

C & A STORE
FOREGATE STREET

This is one of the most successful 20th-century buildings in the city centre. In contrast with many more recent buildings in Foregate Street it has a freshness and honesty of design which has stood the test of time.

Designed by Building Design Partnership, the red brick, black slate, and white

spandrel panels provide the right combination of materials to fit into the Chester vernacular, without overtly copying the half-timbered style. The modelling of the façade is particularly well handled, using a repeating bay feature. The first and second floors overhang the pavement, and the façade is divided into two-bay and four-bay elements separated by a wide access which permitted an existing tree to be retained.

The store received a Civic Trust Commendation in 1972 and remains an excellent example of a modern building that truly enhances the character of a conservation area. C & A ceased trading in Chester in 2000 and the shop was converted to a Woolworths store.

PEPPER STREET CAR PARK

PEPPER STREET

400

1000

1200

1500

1700

1800

1900

*

2000

This multi-storey car park adjacent to the Newgate was designed by The Biggins Sargent Partnership and built on the site of the former Red Lion Brewery. The original design was for a brick-clad building but, following discussion with the Planning Department, it was agreed to echo the aggregate-faced pre-cast concrete panels of the nearby Grosvenor-Laing Precinct. The exterior treatment of the building is an honest expression of its

function; there are shops at ground level on the Pepper Street frontage with levels of car parking above linked by a pedestrian bridge over Park Street to the City Wall.

The original lion, which was a prominent feature of the brewery building, was rescued from the demolition contractor by the then Secretary of The Chester Civic Trust, Dr John Tomlinson, and stored in his garden in Curzon Park. It was re-erected on top of the prominent concrete staircase tower and is an appropriate reminder of the past use of the site which adds interest to the views both from the City Wall and Pepper Street. The lion is believed to be made of 'coadestone', but is not mentioned in Alison Kelly's book on this material.

BELL TOWER

CHESTER CATHEDRAL

Designed by George Pace and named the Addleshaw Tower after the Dean, this was the first detached bell tower to be built for a cathedral in this country since the Reformation.

In the late 1960s the bell frame in the Cathedral's great tower was causing concern and it was decided it would be easier to build a new, detached tower rather than strengthen the existing tower. The Bell Tower is 26 m (85 ft) high and is built of concrete faced with sandstone at the base, whilst the upper part is faced with Bethesda slate.

400
1000
1200
1500
1700
1800
1900
2000

NORTHGATE ARENA

VICTORIA ROAD

This multi-purpose sports arena was built on the site of the former Northgate Railway Station, which closed in 1969. The building, designed by Building Design Partnership, is necessarily large but the careful brick and anodised aluminum detailing enables it to make a positive statement from the inner ring road without being aggressive.

400

1000

1200

1500

1700

1800

1900

2000

1985

SHIPGATE DEVELOPMENT
CASTLE DRIVE AND SHIPGATE STREET

Shipgate is one of the major successes of Chester's conservation programme in that it combines a scheme of restoration with good modern design.

Nowhere in the city was action more urgently required than in the neglected area of Bridgegate. A comprehensive plan was prepared for this area in 1978 by Donald Insall and Associates, including proposals to enable the City and County Councils to tackle the problems in the Shipgate area. The Victorian and Georgian houses on the north side of Shipgate Street were restored and a new property on St Mary's Hill was built. On the south side, a frankly modern scheme for flats and maisonettes was built above a new underground car park. This was designed by James C Sanders, based on a concept proposed by Insalls. Shipgate Street North was commended in the Civic Awards of 1984 and the south side was completed the following year. The assessors commended the developer's initiative and praised the careful attention to materials and detail.

MARKS & SPENCER FINANCIAL SERVICES
WREXHAM ROAD

Designed by Aukett Associates for Marks & Spencer PLC, this was the first building to be erected on the Chester Business Park.

The building sits comfortably on the site with its skilled mounding, planting, and hard landscaping. The brick and glass exterior is consistently well detailed, with the air-conditioning units expressed as vertical features projecting above the flat roof. An inviting entrance leads directly into a central atrium. The building set a standard for the new Business Park which has not been achieved by other buildings erected on the site in the following ten years. It received a RIBA Award in 1990, and Phase 2 was Commended in the Civic Awards of 2000.

400

1000

1200

1500

1700

1800

1900

2000

GROSVENOR COURT

FOREGATE STREET

When the inner ring road was built in the late 1960s, a large traffic island was formed at the eastern end of Foregate Street. Intended for development, this prominent eyesore on the approach to the city centre remained vacant for 20 years, the subject of many abortive schemes. Finally the Colin Stananought Partnership of Chester, acting both as developer and designer, healed the wounds.

The resulting office scheme is a homage to John Douglas (many of whose buildings surround the site), in its concern for good street design as well as for the use of vernacular architectural forms. The offices are built around the perimeter of the island, leaving a protected courtyard at the centre, and each office suite is treated individually, with its own front door. At the corners are larger, Tudor-style blocks in the Douglas manner, connected by neo-Georgian terraces. Unlike other developments in Chester inspired by past styles, the details are carefully considered: sash windows are well-proportioned, and pedimented door cases follow strict precedent. The 'Tudor' blocks are faced in bright red bricks, enlivened by blue brick diapering and stone dressings. Across the road from Grosvenor Court, the Stananought Partnership also converted 117 Foregate Street and built a new extension that curves around the corner to meet the ring road.

This historicist approach to design, often disparagingly referred to as 'pastiche' has acquired a poor image, generally because it compares badly with the original buildings that act as a model. But with Grosvenor Court, it is done very convincingly, and the popular esteem in which it is held in Chester is well deserved.

RUFUS COURT
NORTHGATE STREET

Designed by James Brotherhood and Associates, this award-winning scheme combines conservation and new buildings.

The listed buildings on the perimeter of the site had been empty for many years and, together with the derelict backland, were developed by Rod Cox of the Thompson Cox Partnership to create an intimate courtyard with shops, cafes, offices, a wine bar and flats. This was another scheme promoted by the city's conservation programme which illustrates how undervalued areas of an historic city can be brought to life by small-scale creative intervention, and also how mixed used developments can be made to work successfully.

400
1000
1200
1500
1700
1800
1900
2000

400

1000

1200

1500

1700

1800

1900

2000

1991

CHESTER MAGISTRATES' COURT
GROSVENOR STREET

Occupying a prominent and sensitive location at the junction of Grosvenor Street and the inner ring road, this is one of the most successful 20th-century buildings in the city centre. It was designed by Cheshire County Council's Department of Architecture and replaced inadequate accommodation in Chester Town Hall, where the courts had been held since 1869.

The form of the building is strong and engaging, but without dominance. Its visual success is due to the way the courtrooms are individually expressed,

each with its own separate roof, so that the massing is subtly broken up. The building received a Civic Award in 1995, the assessors commenting that this was 'an outstanding example of a truly modern building fitting well into a historic site'.

THE FORUM AND TJ HUGHES

NORTHGATE STREET/HAMILTON PLACE

'The Forum', dating from the early 1970s, was Chester's most ambitious 20th - century building project. To make way for it, large areas of housing and workshops, and the underlying Roman remains behind the Town Hall were swept away, together with the exuberant façade of the Victorian Market Hall of 1863 and the gothic extension of 1880 which joined it to the Town Hall. Demolition in 1967 left only a fragment of the Market Hall at the southern end. The architects were Michael Lyell Associates of London, who were selected by competition. But the project was never completed: the City gained some council offices, and an intended conference centre became the Gateway Theatre, but the hotel did not get built until 1988, and then to a quite different (and inferior) design.

The labyrinthine car park, the windowless Market Hall, and the claustrophobic shopping mall were never liked, and in 1993 the new owners, Scottish Widows, began a programme of reconstruction. It was to have been done in two phases. The first, designed by Leslie Jones and Partners, involved the removal of the cantilevered brick frontage to the Town Hall Square, and its replacement in 1995 with a bland elevation of stone and glass. More successful is the design of T J Hughes, a new store built off the end of the shopping mall. With its glass lift and blank areas of brickwork, the store elevation facing Hamilton Place relates well to Lyell's original bold office building that it adjoins. Happily, Scottish Widows' second phase was abandoned after they failed to secure planning permission. If current proposals by the new developers London and Amsterdam are carried out, the whole complex will be demolished and replaced by a development designed by Sir Michael Hopkins & Partners.

400

1000

1200

1500

1700

1800

1900

2000

SCOUT HEADQUARTERS
TOWER ROAD

400
1000
1200
1500
1700
1800
1900
2000

This is a building which combines art and architecture and was inspired by Chester's maritime history. The site is at the heart of one of the city's principal regeneration areas - the Old Port of Chester. The architects, Tweed Nuttall Warburton, were also responsible for preparing a masterplan for the first phase of redevelopment, which required the relocation of the Scout Group from a single storey timber building.

The plan, form, and external design are derived from the medieval trading vessels with their high 'stern castles' which frequented the port. Vertical timber boards were fixed to bearing members curved around the steel portal frame and a

clinker planking technique used to form the curved gutters. The profiled white sheeting for the roof evokes sails folded along a boom.

The building is one of three outright winners of the 'Civic Awards 2000' and has been shortlisted in several national award schemes.

St Martins
St Martin's Way

400

1000

1200

1500

1700

1800

1900

*
2000

A large housing development built by Bryant Homes and designed by Jane Derbyshire and David Kendall. It occupies the site of the former Chester Royal Infirmary. The main hospital building fronting City Walls Road, dating from 1761 (*qv*), is currently being converted to apartments, but all the later ward blocks were demolished.

The new housing adopts the densely planned urban layout of the adjoining Georgian enclaves of Stanley Place and King's Buildings, and consists of a mix of terraces and villas, set around small squares and walkways. Fronting St Martin's Way is a tall crescent, which protects the remainder of the development from traffic noise. The buildings are Georgian in spirit, but the details are in the Arts and Crafts tradition, and as a result it avoids the lifeless character of much modern neo-Georgian architecture. In its sensitive layout and contextual design, this scheme not only sets new standards for volume house-building in Chester, but also shows how the horrors of the 1960s ring road can successfully be civilised.

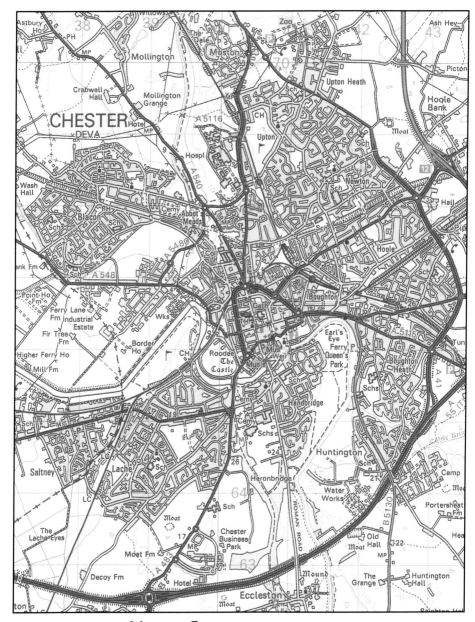

MAP OF CHESTER AS IT IS TODAY

Reproduced from Landranger Sheet 117, 1997, scale 1:50,000, Ordnance Survey map by permission of Ordnance Survey on behalf of the Controller of Her Majesty's Stationery Office.
© Crown Copyright MC 100033853.

CHAPTER 11

CHESTER IN THE 21ST CENTURY
- 'A PROGRESSIVE HISTORIC CITY'?

STEPHEN LANGTREE

You will have noticed that none of the preceding chapters has covered a timespan of less than a hundred years. It seemed a reasonable interval in the context of two thousand years of history, but it is a daunting prospect indeed to extrapolate this forward for another hundred years. How might Chester look in 2100? Will the city's conservation areas be encapsulated within transparent air-conditioned domes? Will a tidal barrier across the Dee protect the lower-lying land from rising sea levels? Will there be any cars? If so, will they be kept on the edges of town; and will a late 20th-century petrol station be part of our collection of preserved historic buildings? Can anyone predict that far ahead, and is it really worth trying?

Before even attempting to look forwards, perhaps we should reflect on the past and try to understand how we have got to where we are now.

We've seen how the invading Romans, Saxons and Normans have each stamped their mark on this country. We can see something of their legacy here in Chester, and we have come to accept their once alien styles of architecture as part of our own heritage. The long metamorphosis has given us many examples of what we now describe as vernacular architecture, particularly from periods such as the Middle Ages when 'local distinctiveness'

was the natural result of relative prosperity and poor communications. Herein lies the first and most instructive clue to the future. Building methods and architectural styles, like culture, fashion and food, are symptomatic of society and its contact with the outside world.

Construction of the turnpikes in the late 17th and early 18th centuries was the first significant advance in communications since the Roman roads were built. The ubiquitous 'Georgian architecture' of the mid 18th century owes as much to better transportation and the opportunities to import materials from further afield as it does to the pursuit of fashion. The advent of the canals later in the 18th century accelerated the movement of materials and components, but it was the arrival of the railways in the mid 19th century which finally brought about the near homogenization of the country.

To its credit, Chester rather 'bucked the trend' in the 1860s by rebelling against the "miserable brick, and incongruous piles of heavy Athenian architecture" which, by then, had pervaded the land. It wasn't long, however, before the city again succumbed to the national pattern with the 20th century seeing several changes of architectural style before another major change of heart.

In fact, as we look back from 2001, it seems clear that no century has witnessed so many changes as the last, and none before that so many as the last but one. Improving communications are bringing ever-increasing rates of change. The process seems to be unstoppable, and whether we like it or not, the only thing constant is change. We're now in a global economy and Chester, like everywhere else, is already being affected by globalisation.

In such circumstances, predictions for one hundred years' time seem quite impossible – and even fifty years presents a challenge. But are we entirely at the mercy of external influences; will we simply react to national and international trends – or is there at least some scope for setting our own agenda? Whilst accepting the limitations, do we at least share a common 'vision' for the future development of Chester? Alas, recent evidence suggests maybe not!

In January 2000 (the first month of what we were all told to accept as the 'new millennium'), two announcements were made in Chester which serve to illustrate the underlying tensions of this so-called "progressive historic city". Both announcements relate to sites outside the City Walls, and both highlight the conflicts which can so easily arise between new development and the preservation of our existing heritage.

The first was the decision by Chester City Council to retain some, but not very much, of the former Chester Electric Lighting Station in New Crane Street. This architecturally undistinguished building dates from 1896 (extended 1900) and occupies a site just beyond the railway viaduct in an area now known, for regeneration purposes, as 'The Old Port of Chester'. It is one of those 'edge-of-centre' areas which has been largely ignored for many years but which has suddenly attracted a great deal of attention and investment. Nothing wrong with that of course! Indeed, the 1990s have seen a rather belated, but no less welcome, recognition of these under-utilised 'brownfield' sites. The Chester Civic Trust's campaign against outward expansion into the Green Belt is, at last, being vindicated in the context of a national trend towards an 'urban renaissance'. The Old Port of Chester certainly has lots of potential for mixed use development and is now benefitting from years of careful masterplanning and targeted investment.

Nevertheless, problems quickly arose from the lack of participation by local residents in the early stages of consultation. So, when the Electric Lighting Station was threatened with demolition to make way for some rather daringly modern office blocks, the locals organised themselves into an effective campaign group. The unlisted Victorian building at the heart of their long and sometimes bitter struggle assumed an importance far beyond its visual qualities or even its historical significance as the birthplace of electricity generation in Chester. Initially it was the focus of community resistance, but soon came to symbolise continuity in a rapidly changing environment.

Chester Electric Lighting Station

After the developer dropped his plans for the offices, Chester City Council commissioned an independent assessment of the merits of the Electric Lighting Station. The original section, which in any case was never anything other than offices, is now being incorporated into a very large new housing scheme – ironically of somewhat less architectural merit than the previously proposed office blocks.

The second announcement (just a few days after Chester Civic Trust's 40th anniversary) re-ignited the longest-running controversy in our historic city for many decades. Surprisingly, Chester's Roman amphitheatre was not discovered until 1929, whereupon it was almost consigned to continuing oblivion by a

Corporation - inspired road improvement scheme. Salvation came only after a very determined campaign by the Chester Archaeological Society in the 1930s which eventually resulted in partial excavation in the 1960s. The amphitheatre has rarely been out of the news ever since and, with only the northern half on public display, it is still regarded by many Cestrians as unfinished business.

In January 2000 David McLean Developments announced that they were about to exercise the planning permission, granted in 1995, to build a new office block on the southern half of the site behind Dee House. The controversial element was that a small part of the new building would overlap the buried remains of the amphitheatre -

and, while founded on a concrete raft to prevent any damage to the underlying archaeology, this will inevitably prevent the full excavation of the Scheduled Ancient Monument.

The public outcry was huge. National attention was briefly focussed on Chester. How could a city with such an established reputation for heritage and conservation allow such a thing to happen? The answers are complex but not altogether convincing. Back in 1995, Chester City Council accepted guidance from English Heritage to the effect that the buried archaeology is 'safe' and should be left for future generations to explore rather than be excavated now. Moreover, as Dee House, a Grade II listed building, already stands on

the site there could be no foreseeable prospect of full excavation. It would not matter therefore if another building were to be added on top of the beleaguered monument. Chester Civic Trust did not agree; we wanted all options to be kept open for the future and asked that the footprint of the new building be modified to avoid any overlap with the amphitheatre. Unfortunately, the Council didn't listen, the developer didn't listen and, six years later, many Cestrians are looking forward to the demolition of a new County Court building which has only just been opened!

There are some striking contradictions in these two cases, but also some depressingly common features. In retrospect one can identify a lack of foresight on the part of

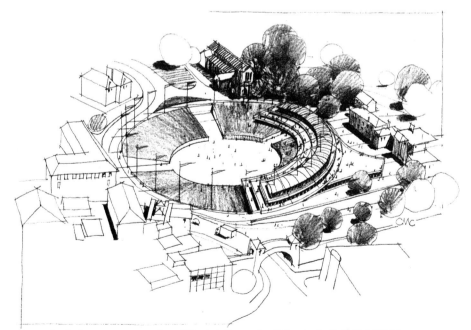

Concept for the long-term presentation of Chester's Roman Amphitheatre by Stephen Langtree (Chairman of The Chester Civic Trust). Drawing by Clive McWilliam, May 2000

Chester City Council, coupled with a somewhat grudging attitude towards local opinion. More importantly, these examples illustrate the strength of public feeling for our links with the past. Although membership of amenity societies such as the Civic Trust is not unusually high in Chester, there can be no doubt that a great many local people have very strong views about their city. Sadly, the manifestation of public opinion is all too often reactive rather than proactive, but that should not diminish its significance. Those who control the destiny and development of our historic city should not underestimate the strength of public opinion and should heed the Government's advice to harness this interest in pursuit of a more open agenda for the future.

At the same time, Cestrians, old and new, need to be a lot more constructive and proactive. If this city is as special as we all like to think it is, then it's up to each section of the community - public, private and voluntary - to work in partnership to avoid such conflicts and to define a common vision for Chester in the 21st century.

Chester Civic Trust, for its part, has always adopted a very positive and sometimes pioneering role in urban initiatives and environmental improvements. We have a 'Vision for Chester', but we know that we are not alone. There are people and organisations throughout the city with their own vision of the future. Our councillors and local authority officers are even now working hard to draw together all the strands into a common vision defined by the Community Plan. The Civic Trust is making a contribution to Chester's 'urban design strategy' and will, no doubt, continue to promote high quality and sustainability above short-term expediency. We have never got as far as thinking about Chester in fifty or a hundred years' time, but we are convinced of the need to set our own agenda - even if it has to be in the context of burgeoning national and global trends.

Above all, we must be open to change. If nothing else, this book demonstrates that change will happen whether we wish it or not.

That said, there ought to be a consensus on how things should change and which features should be protected against it. The essence of Donald Insall's conservation study in 1968 was "to provide guidance for continuing change". So, we need a framework; and, with lots of good material already to hand, it doesn't have to be a new one every ten years!

We should examine the existing analyses of Chester's townscape, recognise the importance of 'human scale', celebrate the variety of architectural styles, the intricacy of detail and, above all, preserve the harmony of our townscape. New buildings should always be allowed in the right circumstances - but they must be good, both in their own right and as neighbours to our existing treasures.

And how shall we use this evolving building stock – for more shops, for offices, for city centre apartments .... for whatever 'the market' demands? Well, no! The start of a new millennium could, and should, be a defining moment when we try to set our own agendas for the future.

Maybe we are already in danger of setting off in the wrong direction. The current 'Northgate' scheme seems likely to be over-dominated by multiple retailing in what must surely be a vain attempt to challenge 'Cheshire Oaks', the 'Trafford Centre' and other out-of-town emporia. Of course, shops are important, as are all the basic necessities of life at affordable prices, but Chester doesn't have to be the same as everywhere else. This city is, as we know, both different and distinctive. We have a very special environment, a unique system of Rows, a large (if somewhat depleted) number of small specialist shops and a hard-earned reputation for quality and service. These are the things which should be encouraged and promoted if we want our city to thrive in an increasingly competitive market.

Chester also needs to develop its heritage attractions rather more than it has done already. We've got a Castle which no-one goes to, towers on the City Walls which are rarely open and an amphitheatre which (despite the recent set-back) still has so much untapped potential. We do not seem to be making the most of our historical assets – and this complacency could be our undoing.

There is an urgent need for a complete review of Chester's heritage assets and a business plan for future investment, development and management. The city (badly) needs a new Visitor Centre, more modern means of heritage interpretation, new attractions for families and much greater use of its parks and open spaces.

In fact, Chester needs a fresh impetus: one which builds on the achievements of the conservation programme, takes advantage of the city's commercial strength, and consolidates the current investment in urban regeneration. It's not enough to just build more shops! The 'Northgate' scheme presents both challenges and opportunities, but elsewhere in the city centre there are other sites with immediate potential to launch Chester into the 21st century.

The Amphitheatre, with a state-of-the-art Visitors' Centre (alongside Souters Lane), would be the ideal starting point for everyone to explore our 2000 years of history. The Castle, having two large buildings currently vacant, could be part of a new 'cultural quarter' embracing the existing Museums, providing gallery space, craft workshops and restaurants, and linking to a spectacular new hotel, conference centre and concert venue on the site of the former Police Headquarters. The Racecourse also has potential – not on the visually critical 'greenspace' – but on the land adjoining New Crane Street. And then there's Gorse Stacks, Commonhall Street, Tower Wharf and 'The Old Port' – not to mention the potential swathe of redevelopment between Boughton and the Railway Station.

Culture (of all types), conferences, history, heritage and shopping – all in a clean, well-presented city served by modern, efficient public transport. All this, and more, amidst the most wonderful architectural legacy imaginable. If these opportunities are recognised and acted upon, then Chester really could begin to set its own agenda for the 21st century - providing an unsurpassed urban experience for residents and visitors alike.

SOURCES

History of the City of Chester,
Hemingway, J., 2 vols., J. Fletcher,
Chester, 1831.

The Chester Guide,
Roberts, H., Chester, 1851, reprinted by
Chester Archives, 1996.

The Stranger's Handbook to Chester,
Hughes, T., Thomas Catherall, Chester,
1856, reprinted by E.J. Morton,
Manchester, 1972.

Chester: A Study in Conservation,
D.W. Insall & Associates,
HMSO, London, 1968.
(Known as 'The Insall Report')

The Buildings of England: Cheshire,
Pevsner, N., & Hubbard, E., Penguin
Books, Harmondsworth, 1971.

Victorian & Edwardian Chester,
Tomlinson, J., Deesider Publications,
Chester, 1976.

Bartholomew City Guide to Chester,
Harris, B.E., John Bartholomew & Son
Ltd, Edinburgh & London, 1979.

Conservation in Action: Chester's
Bridgegate,
Insall, D.W., and Department of the
Environment, HMSO, London, 1982.

Loyal Chester,
Kennett, A., (ed.), Chester City Record
Office, Chester, 1984.

Galleries Which They Call the Rows,
Chester Archaeological Society, 1985.

Georgian Chester,
Kennett, A., (ed.), Chester City Record
Office, Chester, 1987.

Conservation in Chester,
Insall, D.W., & Morris, C.M.,
Chester City Council, 1988.

Mrs Coade's Stone,
Kelly, A., The Self Publishing Association,
Upton-upon-Severn, 1990.

The Work of John Douglas,
Hubbard, E., The Victorian Society,
London, 1991.

The Buildings of Chester,
Morriss, R.K., & Hoverd, K., Alan Sutton
Publishing Ltd, Stroud, 1993.

Book of Chester,
Carrington, P., English Heritage & B.T.
Batsford, London, 1994.

Miller of Dee: the Story of Chester's Mills,
Wilding, R., Gordon Emery, Chester,
1997.

Picturesque Chester,
Boughton, P.J., Phillimore & Co. Ltd,
Chichester, 1997.

A History of the Civil Parish of Great
Boughton, Cheshire,
Wright, C.F., Great Boughton Parish
Council, 1997.

The Rows of Chester,
Brown, A. (ed.), English Heritage,
London, 1999.

Chester Archaeological Society, the First
One Hundred and Fifty Years,
Crosby, A., Chester Archaeological
Society, Chester, 1999.

Chester Castle Conservation Plan,
Donald Insall Associates, Giffords and
The Architectural History Practice,
prepared for English Heritage, 2001.

ACKNOWLEDGEMENTS

This book was conceived by Stephen Langtree, Chairman of the Chester Civic Trust, as part of the city's Millennium celebrations.

Planning was undertaken by members of the Festival Partnership and funding was provided by **The Westminster Foundation**, for which the Trust is particularly grateful.

In addition to the principal authors named in the Contents, the following people also contributed sections of the text: Peter Brigham, Alan Comyns, Stephen Langtree, Mike Mercer and Graeme White.

Most of the photographs were taken by the following members of the Chester Photographic Survey, which was established in 1963 to keep a systematic record of the changing face of our city:

Tom Hand	*(TH)*
Stephen Langtree	*(SL)*
Len Morgan	*(LM)*
Derek Nuttall	*(DN)*
Mike Penney	*(MP)*
Allan Pullin	*(AVP)*
Keith Truman	*(KT)*
John Wolfenden	*(JLW)*

Chester Civic Trust is greatly indebted to all the above for their skill, co-operation and generous contributions to this book.

We also wish to thank the following people and organisations who have contributed the remaining photographs:

(the late) David Baldwin	*(DB)*
Peter Brigham	*(PB)*
Chester College	*(CC)*
The Grosvenor Museum	*(GM)*
Kerry Maddrell	*(KM)*
John Mills Photography Ltd	*(JMP)*
Michael Reed ARPS	*(MR)*
Diana Skilbeck	*(DS)*
Tim Strickland	*(TJS)*
John W Warren	*(JWW)*
Simon Warburton	*(SW)*

We thank David Mason for providing his plan of the Roman legionary fortress in AD 235 (page 16).

Oliver Bott drew the sketches used in the Introduction to Chapter 5; Chester Education provided the plans which illustrate Chapter 2 (with acknowledgement to Cheshire County Council's Advisory & Inspection Service), and most of the other maps, drawings and sketches have been reproduced by kind permission of Chester Archaeology or other departments of Chester City Council.

Polly Bird provided administrative assistance and Don McIntyre helped with the proof-reading.

The book was designed and typeset by **Kerry Maddrell Design Services**.
Printing was by **The Printing House Ltd.**

INDEX

A

Abbey	49
Abbey Gateway	70
Abbey Square	120
Abbey Square, Nos 13, 14	99
Abbey Street	122
Addleshaw's Tower	206
Agricola's tower	55
Albion Hotel	109, 112
Albion Inn	160
Albion Street	160
Amphitheatre	25, 220
Anchorite's Cell	80
Aukett Associates	209
Ayrton, Maxwell	195

B

Bains, G Grenfell	182, 202
Bath Street, Nos 1-11, 13	184
Baths, public	178
Baths, Roman	22
Bear & Billet	90, 104
Bell Tower	206
Benson's at the Billet	104
Beswick, H	179, 187
Biggins Sargent Partnership	135, 205
Bishop Lloyd's Palace	96
Bishop's Palace	118
Blue Bell	86
Blue Coat School	114
Bonewaldesthorne's Tower	74
Bookland's crypt	81
Boot Inn	87
Booth Mansion	66
Boughton Grange	116
Boughton Hall	100

Boughton Lodge	116
Brassey, Thomas	150, 151, 156
Bridge of Sighs	126
Bridgegate	132
Bridge House	107
Bridge Place	124
Bridge Street, No 43	102
Britannia Inn	95
Britton, S E	190
Brotherhood, James & Assocs.	136, 146, 211
Browns of Chester	147
Browns' crypt	71
Building Design Partership	182, 202, 204, 207
Bullivant, R	196
Burgess, H	178

C

C & A Store	204
Canal	125
Canal cutting	126
Castle	40, 134, 143
Cathedral	49
Chapter House	51
Cherry Orchard	116
Chester Canal	125
Chester Cathedral	49
Chester City Club	142
Chester College Chapel	148
Chester Library	191
Chester General Railway Station	150
Chester Magistrates' Court	212
Chester Royal Infirmary	123
Christ Church	173
City Baths	178
City Club	142

City Gaol	126
City Walls	46
Civil war	48, 89, 100
Clegg, H A	176
Cole, W,	145, 164
Colin Stananought Partnership	210
Commercial Hotel/Inn	142
Commercial Newsroom	142
Common Hall	73
Coniston	176
Constabulary Headquarters	203
County Hall	199
Cowper House	81
Cross Buildings, The	170
Crosses, Saxon	35
Custom House Inn, Ye Olde	101

D

Davies, J H & Sons	185
Dee Bridge	84
Dee House	117
Derby House	94
Derby Place	149
Derbyshire, J	215
Deva Terrace	152
District Bank	181, 192
Domesday Book	37
Donald Insall & Associates	65, 124, 182, 171, 208
Douglas, John	45, 162, 164-168, 173-175, 177-179, 181, 184
Drill Hall	160, 161
Dutch Houses	106

E

Eastgate	177
Eastgate clock	177
Eastgate Street, Nos 28-34	147
Eastgate Street, No 33	156
Edgar, Ye Olde	93

Edgar's Cave	29
Egerton House	181, 202
Electric Lighting Building	218, 219
Eliptical Building	17
Ellesmere Canal	125, 127

F

Falcon Inn	64
Feathers Inn	23
Filkin's Lane	116
Forest House	129
Forum, The	213
Frost, F A & Sons	146

G

Gamul House	92
Gardeners Arms, Ye	185
Georgian Chester	109
George & Dragon	194
Gerrard, E	154, 193
God's Providence House	158
Gregan, J E	148
Grosvenor Bridge	145
Grosvenor Club (Eastgate Street)	167
Grosvenor Club (Vicars lane)	119
Grosvenor Court	210
Grosvenor Hotel	14
Grosvenor Laing Precinct	200
Grosvenor Museum	169
Grosvenor Park Road	166
Grosvenor Precinct	200
Grosvenor Shopping Centre	201

H

Hamilton Place	24
Harrison, James	73, 79, 154, 155, 158
Harrison, Thomas	55, 134, 142-145
Hartley, J	145
Hermitage	80
Hopkins, Sir Michael	213

HSBC Bank	167
Hughes, T J	213
Hydro-electric station	190
Hypocaust	22, 23

I

Infirmary	123

J

James Brotherhood & Associates	136, 146, 211
Jiggins, A H F	202
Johnson, S	135
Jones, F	192
Jones, T	173

K

Kendall, D	215
King Charles' Tower	57, 69
King's Buildings	128
King Street	128
King's Head Hotel	63
Kirby, E	117

L

Leadworks	137, 146
Leche House	82
Legionary headquarters	24
Leslie Jones & Parners	213
Library	191
Lockwood, Philip H	191
Lockwood, Thomas M	96, 159, 163, 169-171
Lockwood, William T	188
Lovejoy & Partners, Derek	203
Love Street School	187
Lower Park Road	154
Lynn, W H	159

M

Magistrates' Court	212
Manor House	116
Marks & Spencer Financial Services	209
Mathew Henry's Chapel	181
Michael Lyell Associates	213
Midland Bank	167
Mill of Dee	54
Miln's Seeds	146
Minerva shrine	29
Mitchell, W	203
Museum	169
Music Hall	73

N

NatWest Bank	156
Nesfield, W E	163
Newgate	198
Newsroom	142
Nicholas Street	131
Nicholson, Sir Charles	173
Nine Houses	103
Norman Chester	37
North & South Wales Bank	167
Northgate	126
Northgate Arena	207
Northgate Locks	127

O

Oddfellows' Hall	107
Odeon Cinema	196
Old Bank Buildings	140
Old Bishop's Palace	118
Old Custom House Inn	101
Old Dee Bridge	84
Olde Edgar	93
Old Kings Head	63
Old Rectory, Bridge Street	102
Old Rectory, Vicar's Lane	119
Ould, E A L	168
Overleigh Cemetery	176

P

Pace, G	206
Paparazzi Ristorante	155
Park House	112
Parker's Buildings	172
Parkes, E M	199
Penson, T M	139, 147, 157
Pepper Street car park	205
Percy Thomas & Son	200
Phoenix Tower	57, 69
Pied Bull Hotel	98
Police Headquarters	203
Potts, H	144
Prudential Assurance Building	184

Q

Quay (Roman)	28
Queen Commercial Hotel	157
Queen Hotel	157
Queen's Park Suspension Bridge	193
Queen's School, The	168

R

Railway Station	150
Roman amphitheatre	25
Roman baths	22
Roman Chester	17
Roman hypocaust	22, 23
Roman legionary headquarters	24
Roman quay wall	28
Roman walls	20
Rowell, David, & Co Ltd	193
Rows	60
Royal Bank of Scotland	192
Royal Infirmary	123
Rufus Court	211

S

Salmon Leap	54
Sanders, J C	208
Sandown Terrace	153
Saxon Chester	31
Saxon crosses	35
Saxon Smith & Partners	192
Scott, Sir George Gilbert	14, 53, 140
Scott, Sir Giles Gilbert	199
Scout Headquarters	214
Sealand Road Church	186
Sedan House	130
Seddon, J P	79
Shipgate House	113
Shipgate Development	208
Shoemakers' Row	179
Shot Tower	137
Shuttleworth's crypt	75
St John's Church	43
St John's Rectory	119
St Martins	215
St Martin's Gate	202
St Mary on the Hill	79
St Michael's Arcade	188
St Michael's Row	188
St Nicholas's Chapel	73
St Paul's Church	164
St Peter's Church	78
St Peter's Churchyard	142
St Werburgh's Mount	162
St Werburgh Street, Nos 2-18	174
St Werburgh Row	195
Stanley Palace	94
Stanley Place	110, 130
Star Inn	201
Steam Mill	146
Strong, J	179
Suspension Bridge	193
Sweet shop	163

T

Taberner, E	203
Talbot Hotel	112
Tapper, Sir W and M	198
Taylor's boatyard	127
Telford, Thomas	136, 145
Telford's Warehouse	136
Theatre Royal	73
Thomas, Percy & Son	200
Thompson Cox Partnership	211
Thompson, F	140, 150
Three Old Arches	68
Tin Tabernacle	186
TJ Hughes' Store	213
Town Crier	157
Town Hall	159
Trustee Savings Bank	155
Tudor House	95
Turner, J	131, 132, 133
Tweed Nuttall Warburton	214

U

Uffington House	168

V

Vicar's Lane	43, 119
Victorian Chester	139

W

Walls	20-21, 46-48
Walmoor Hill	175
Water Tower	74
Watergate	133
Watergate House	144
Watergate Street, Nos 38-42	76-77
Watergates' Wine Bar	72
Weedon, H	196
Weir	54
Westminster Coach & Motor Car Works	191
Wild, C H	150
Williams, G	156
Wolfgate	198
Woolworths Store	204

Y

Ye Gardners Arms	185
Ye Olde Custom House Inn	101
Ye Olde Edgar	93
Ye Olde Kings Head	63
YMCA (former)	118

About the Editors.....

Stephen Langtree is a chartered civil engineer with international consultants Binnie Black & Veatch. A Lancastrian (by birth), Cumbrian (by upbringing) and now Cestrian (by adoption), his long-standing interest in heritage and the built environment may stem from an unfulfilled ambition to take a second degree in Town Planning. Stephen joined Chester Civic Trust in 1986, was Hon Secretary for four years, Chairman for eight years and is now a Vice President.

Dr Alan Comyns is an industrial chemical consultant, author of a dictionary of named chemical processes. He has been interested in architecture and archaeology for many years; a member of the Council of The Chester Civic Trust 1996-2001; currently Chairman of the Chester Archaeological Society.